...ryday Living in Later
...

Edited by Bill Bytheway

NUMBER 4 IN

**THE REPRESENTATION OF OLDER PEOPLE
IN AGEING RESEARCH SERIES**

THE CENTRE FOR POLICY ON AGEING AND
THE CENTRE FOR AGEING AND BIOGRAPHICAL
STUDIES AT THE OPEN UNIVERSITY

SERIES EDITORS
SHEILA PEACE AND JOANNA BORNAT

The Open
University

First published in 2003
by the Centre for Policy on Ageing
19-23 Ironmonger Row
London EC1V 3QP
Tel: +44 (0)20 7553 6500
Fax: +44 (0)20 7553 6501
Email: cpa@cpa.org.uk
Website: www.cpa.org.uk

Registered charity no 207163

British Library Cataloguing in Publication Data
A catalogue record for this book is available from the British Library

ISBN 1 901097 70 6

The representation of Older People in Ageing Research Series is based on
seminars organised by the Centre for Ageing and Biographical Studies, School of
Health and Social Welfare, The Open University, and the Centre for Policy on
Ageing. The fourth seminar was held in London on 2 March 2001.

Also available in the series:

Biographical Interviews: the link between research and practice, edited by Joanna
Bornat (No 1)
*Involving Older People in Research: "An amateur doing the work of a
professional?"*, edited by Sheila Peace (No 2)
Writing Old Age (No 3) – forthcoming

*Printed in the United Kingdom by Henry Ling Limited,
at the Dorset Press, Dorchester, DT1 1HD*

CONTENTS

1   INTRODUCTION: STORIES OF 'EVERYDAY LIVING IN LATER LIFE'

KEN PLUMMER   1

2   INTERPRETING MEASURES OF ACTIVITIES OF DAILY LIVING

JANET ASKHAM   8

3   A DAY IN THE LIFE: INTERPRETING FIRST HAND ACCOUNTS FROM THE MASS-OBSERVATION ARCHIVE

DOROTHY SHERIDAN AND CAROLINE HOLLAND   20

4   EVERY DAY'S THE SAME? A STUDY OF THE MANAGEMENT OF LONG-TERM MEDICATION

BILL BYTHEWAY AND JULIA JOHNSON   34

5   THE USE OF DIARIES TO STUDY THE EVERYDAY FOOD LIFE OF OLDER PEOPLE

ANGELA DICKINSON   49

1

INTRODUCTION
STORIES OF 'EVERYDAY LIVING IN LATER LIFE'

KEN PLUMMER

The four papers, which are collected here, were originally presented at a day seminar in London in March 2001, organised jointly by the Centre for Ageing and Biographical Studies at the Open University, and the Centre for Policy on Ageing.

The seminar addressed the following questions:

- How should we research the routines of everyday living?

- How significant is the difference between what actually happens and what older people say usually happens?

- How should we interpret anecdotes, e.g. about what happened only last week?

- How can we place evidence in the broader context of the experience of age and ageing?

At the heart of the four papers lies a dual concern. First, they start to explore themes regarding the mundane nature of everyday ageing life, an area that has been explored empirically but which is still lacking in theoretical studies of ageing. Secondly, they all use qualitative tools of documentary research – diaries, letters, logs, etc. – that enable the first hand recording of these experiences. Table 1 provides a brief summary of how they approach these issues.

THE MUNDANE EXPERIENCE OF AGEING LIFE

Just how do older people get through their days? How do they live their everyday lives?

In general, this is an area that only a few social scientists have focused upon – the mundane processes of getting up, getting washed, eating and drinking, and ultimately just 'getting through the day'. The papers

Table 1: The research projects in summary

	Themes	*Tools*
Janet Askham	Rethinking the General Household Survey's measures of ADLs – 'Activities of Daily Living' Body management in everyday living	Critique of ADLs via two studies: (a) Interviews and observations around dementia, (b) Interviews with people over 85 living independently
Dorothy Sheridan and Caroline Holland	Wide ranging. All kinds of everyday life experiences, though often organised through a call for essays by themes (e.g. gay family life)	Mass-Observation Archive, rich in data from over-fifties. Data from letters, essays, emails – personal documents
Bill Bytheway and Julia Johnson	Medication use and regimes	Critical use and evaluation of the 'diary-diary interview' with representative sample
Angela Dickinson	Everyday food life of older people	24 'free-living' over-sixties' 'food diaries' as part of 'diary-diary interviews'

in this monograph all speak to this mundane quality of the doing of everyday life. Janet Askham looks at daily activities, Angela Dickinson at feeding, Bill Bytheway and Julia Johnson at long-term medication, and Dorothy Sheridan and Caroline Holland at more general experiences of daily living.

In sum, they focus on the very mundane concerns of daily life – touching on the ways in which the body is managed, and how older people 'mooch and amble' through the day. With age, regular daily benchmarks such as work come to an end and enormous significance starts to be given to the care of the body, medical regimes, eating and sleeping, as well routine shopping. This book starts to address such concerns.

But there are critical problems here that need to be taken further. Janet Askham, for example, looks at the work of the General Household Survey and how it tries to measure Activities of Daily Living (ADLs). She finds it wanting. For, although these measurements do indeed centre on mundane issues like feeding, dressing, and the handling of medications, she offers a largely critical treatment of this approach because of its over-emphasis on tasks and task management, and its over-concern with the simplicity, routine and narrowness of such everyday processes.

I would take her critical comments even further. What is needed is a concern to theorise more adequately the day-to-day strategies through which people make sense of their lives. There is now a significant body of writing that examines the nature of 'everyday life' from a number of angles. Through Freud there is a concern with the psychopathology of everyday life. Erving Goffman's work houses a classic interest with the ways in which the self is presented in everyday encounters. Stan Cohen and Laurie Taylor have examined the psychological strategies deployed by largely middle class people to just make it through the day with a whole series of resistances.

Table 2 lists some of the key books on everyday life which provide foundations for further studies of ageing and everyday life. With few exceptions, however, this is a topic which has not been applied to the social worlds of older people.

Table 2: Some resources for the study of the mundane nature of everyday ageing life

---

Sigmund Freud: *The Psychopathology of Everyday Life*

Leon Trotsky: *Problems of Everyday Life*

Erving Goffman: *The Presentation of Self in Everyday Life*

Michael de Certeau: *The Practices of Everyday Life*

Marcello Truzzi: *Sociology and Everyday Life*

Stan Cohen and Laurie Taylor: *Escape Attempts: The Theory and Practice of Resistance in Everyday Life*

Henri Lefebre: *Everyday Life in the Modern World*

Candace West: *Misery and Company: Sympathy in Everyday Life*

Sarah Nettleton and Jonathan Watson: *The Body in Everyday Life*

Shaun Moores: *Media and Everyday Life in Modern Society*

Barry Glassner: *Qualitative Sociology as Everyday Life*

Jorg Durrschmidt: *Everyday Lives in the Global City*

John Ross: *Living Dangerously: Navigating the Risks of Everyday Life*

Thomas Moore: *Care of the Soul: A Guide for Cultivating Depth and Sacredness in Everyday Life*

Joan Cleveland: *Simplifying Life as a Senior Citizen: Hundreds of Tips for Everyday Living*

Jaber Gubrium and James Holstein: *Ageing and Everyday Life*

David Karp: *Sociology in Everyday Life*

TELLING THE MUNDANE EXPERIENCE OF AGEING LIFE: FROM PERSONAL DOCUMENTS TO 'AGEING NARRATIVES'

A second prime concern of the papers is to address the ways in which everyday life gets recorded and narrated. All the studies use what have been called personal documents or what I have termed 'documents of life' (Plummer 2001). These are methodologies that are immensely valuable yet, until recently, seriously underused and neglected in social science. Yet in these four papers we can find the classic use of (a) life story interviews, alongside a strong focus on (b) the use of the diary and the log: with keeping a record of the day-to-day life and its events, and (c) the use of personal testimonies – mainly in the celebrated collection of the Mass-Observation Archive, with its emerging blended 'genre' (as Dorothy Sheridan and Caroline Holland say) drawing upon 'family letter, school essay, newspaper report, personal diary, testimony, confessional and so on'.

The kinds of accounts presented here are usually seen to be valid. If you want to know about how older people live their lives, then getting close to them through their own diaries and voices must surely be one of the better ways. But when it comes to matters of reliability and representativeness, such documents are not always considered so valuable. For instance, with representativeness, we need to engage with full-scale sampling theory. Thus it may be that we have a rather oddball group of people in these papers – the really poor may have gone missing as may the really rich. Likewise, those who are functioning very well may be under-represented. We need to know.

Nevertheless, what these methods do so well is tap into the daily flow of life experiences. But as is remarked, these are not actual flows of life but life as it is narrated. All the documents used here then are also social constructions and, as such, questions need to be posed around not just what is said but how such things come to be said, like this, here in this text. They are documentations, matters of record, textual constructions; and like all such constructions they do pose problems. What is needed now is a concern with how people tell the stories of their lives, for whom, why, where, when, and with what consequences.

Thus it is becoming increasingly the task of researchers of ageing and everyday life to also ask questions such as:

- What warrant do I have to get older people to tell me the story of their lives?

- What resources do they draw upon in telling me of their lives?

- How are their lives fashioned into a narrative – what conventions of narrative writing help in this telling?

- What is not being told? And why?

As part of a wider 'narrative turn', social gerontologists are increasingly showing a fascination with the life story metaphor and the idea of ageing narratives. Hearing the stories told by older people are becoming more and more important – not just as reminiscences and oral histories, fields now well established through such pioneering works as those of Joanna Bornat and Paul Thompson (Bornat 1994; Thompson *et al.* 1990), but as modes in which *the composing of a life actually tends towards giving a shape to the life* – to making sense of it all. Through 'guided autobiography' (Birren *et al.* 1996), the core themes of a life can be constructed, an 'autobiographical memory' (Kenyon and Randall 1997) sensed, and a kind of overview of the life provided which can provide senses of self. Increasingly though we should not be expecting grand stories about these lives – stories which are linear, forceful and suggest lives well led and coherently driven. Rather instead, we should be looking at these narratives as inchoate patchworks, as fragmented archipelagos. Jaber Gubrium (1975), for instance, whilst listening to the life stories of the residents of *Murray Manor* can sense, tellingly, that many lives never achieve a coherence – that many 'elderly faces' may reveal the fragments of stories past, whilst being unable to find connections with (an often diseased) present. As he says at the close of his book of life stories:

> There is little overall evidence that affairs are ultimately settled, sundered ties finally repaired, transgressions at last righted or accounted for, or preparations of the future or the afterlife completed. (Gubrium 1993: 188)

THE FUTURE: THE POSTMODERNISATION OF AGEING AND AGEING STUDIES

At the beginning of the twenty-first century, social research finds itself on the brink of new ways of speaking and writing the lives of others. What might be called 'Classical Social Science Texts' with their introduction, literature review, 'methods', findings, discussion, conclusion, notes and bibliography, may be on their way out for more critical thinkers. Such texts are machine-like, written for highly specialised audiences, with all the accruements of 'academia'.

Yet to suggest doing it any other way is often to be seen as frivolous, non-academic and indulgent. But why should there be only the one approved way to present social science material? And why, indeed, if this is always an elitist and non-populist mode? It seems to me that increasingly the human sciences should face the daunting task of learning how to communicate in more popular and accessible ways.

There has been a narrowness in the way we think about producing our work, and new forms should be experimented with and – where they work well – they should be added on to the sociological imagination at work: taught, studied, debated and used. The core concerns are to recognise ourselves in and around our research; to see that the presentation of it really matters; and to jolt both author and reader (in almost Brechtian ways) to rethink, and rethink again, just what it is they are doing.

Amongst the new and experimental ways of expressing everyday life in research are the use of photographs, video, video diaries, personal narrative, auto/ethnography, experimental ethnography, as dramatising the text. But it can also mean more closely studying the performativities of life: Anne Davis Basting studied 'old age' through eight different theatrical productions where older people actually set about constructing their own unique meanings of old age (Basting 1998).

REFERENCES

Basting, A.D. (1998) *The Stages of Age: Performing Age in Contemporary American Culture*, University of Michigan Press, Ann Arbor.

Birren, J.E., Kenyon, G.M., Ruth, J-E., Schroots, J. and Svensson, T. (eds) (1996) *Aging and Biography: Explorations in Adult Development*, Springer, New York.

Bornat, J. (ed.) (1994) *Reminiscence Reviewed: Perspectives, Evaluations, Achievements*, Open University Press, Buckingham.

Gubrium, J.F. (1975) *Living and Dying at Murray Manor*, St. Martin's Press, New York.

Gubrium, J.F. (1993) *Speaking of Life: Horizons of Meaning for Nursing Home Residents*, Aldine de Gruyter, New York.

Gubrium, J.F. and Holstein, J.A. (2000) *Aging and Everyday Life*, Blackwell Publishers, Oxford.

Kenyon, G.M. and Randall, W.M. (1997) *Restorying Our Lives: Personal Growth Through Autobiographical Reflection*, Praeger, Westport CT.

Thompson, P., Itzin, K. and Abendstern, M. (1990) *I Don't Feel Old: the Experience of Later Life*, Oxford University Press, Oxford.

Plummer, K. (2001) *Documents of Life: An Invitation to a Critical Humanism – 2*, Sage, London.

2

INTERPRETING MEASURES OF ACTIVITIES OF DAILY LIVING

JANET ASKHAM

INTRODUCTION

This paper is a reflection on some of the differences between what older people say when questioned in surveys about their everyday lives and what they say when asked to talk more spontaneously about them. Its starting point is the British General Household Survey (the GHS), which has on several occasions included questions to older sample members about 'activities of daily life' (ADLs). It is interesting to note that these concepts are not categories used in everyday language; we do not have ADLs as identified by the GHS in our everyday speech:

> ... people aged 65 and over taking part in the GHS were asked a series of questions about the activities and tasks they undertook and whether they needed help to perform them. These questions measure Activities of Daily Living (ADLs), which have been defined as tasks which people need to be able to perform to survive without help, and Instrumental Activities of Daily Living (IADLs) which are those which are necessary for living a more-or-less normal life without help. (Bridgwood 2000)

As is well known to those who use the GHS, ADLs are taken to mean activities like feeding oneself, going to the lavatory, moving from bed to chair, dressing and bathing. IADLs include activities such as using a telephone, shopping, food preparation, housekeeping, laundry, travel, handling one's medication and one's finances. Such measures are said to be useful at a population level 'to calculate healthy active life expectancy' (Bridgwood 2000: 14). Based on the lowest rungs of Maslow's 'hierarchy of needs' (Maslow 1987), they may be useful at this basic level, but do they tell us much about the everyday lives of older people? Are these really the activities which people need to perform to survive? Is asking these questions the best way of finding out if people do these activities? Is what they say what they actually do in their everyday lives?

In this paper I shall take a few of these kinds of activity and examine them a little more closely using for purposes of illustration excerpts from interviews with older people from two of our recent research projects: an observation and interview study of how care for older people with dementia is actually carried out at home (Askham *et al.* 1998), and an interview study of people aged 85 and over living independently at home (Tinker *et al.* 2000). First it may be useful to look a little more closely at the GHS questions themselves, which were most recently asked of people aged 65 and over in 1998/99. They were introduced (immediately after a question on 'eyesight difficulties and/or activities being limited by ill health or disability') as follows:

> Now I'd like to ask about a few tasks that some people may be able to do on their own, while others may need help, or not do them at all. For some tasks I will ask you to look at these cards and tell me whether you usually manage to do it on your own, only with help from someone else, or not at all.

What is interesting about this statement is that:

- it appears to imply that the activities to be asked about are 'tasks'

- it appears to imply that they are things one does or does not 'manage' to do, rather than just things one does or cannot do (an implication which someone of 65 – or even 75 – might well find insulting)

- the word 'usually' is used without any further explanation

And when one comes to look at the actual questions, further things strike one:

- They suggest to some extent that people's lives are lived largely within their own home environment (witness the question 'Do you have to use stairs to get from the rooms you use during the daytime to your bedroom?'). In other words there is an assumption that the life of older people is narrow and home-confined. It presents a certain image of later life which respondents are expected to understand and go along with.

- It is assumed that life is an existence of routine sameness; for example, that whether things are easy or difficult does not vary from day to day or hour to hour.

- It is assumed that if people have help it is human agency help, and that if they have such help there is a 'usual' helper. Also there seems to be an assumption that 'being able to manage on one's own with great difficulty' and having a 'helper/carer' are two points on the same continuum, with the latter being further along than the former. But this is probably not the case; people in the former category include those who would have help but who happen not to have anyone available to help them.

- It is assumed that activities are straightforward, simple or homogeneous (or rather that respondents will know what part of a complex series of actions they are expected to be thinking about in answering the question); for instance, when asking about whether 'you can feed yourself' or 'use public transport'.

- It is assumed that inability to manage is due to the health or disability of the respondent and not to the environment, as can be seen by the final crunch question, designed to be a check on what has gone before: 'Do you need regular daily help with things that fit and healthy people would normally do for themselves?'

- The ADL questions are supposed to be activities necessary for survival without help. Yet independent survival depends not just on caring for one's body, but also on caring for one's safety in the environment.

There is of course research on the validity of ADL/IADL questions. For example in the MRC Cognitive Function and Ageing Study (which uses them), a paper describes research by Kelly-Hayes *et al.* (1992) which found that:

> when a self-reported scale was compared with an objectively measured scale using the same items ... (the authors) 'reported higher disability in self-rating scale, with more disparities with increasing age and poorer cognitive function'.

McGee *et al.* (1998) go on to say that: 'Here self-reported measures may reflect past rather than current ability and could be accounted for by either cognitive decline or, for subjects living at home, self-perceived concern that the questionnaire is an assessment of their ability to live at home.' This is useful in demonstrating that what people say may not be what they do but, if we want to examine the concepts more broadly, different kinds of study are needed. In the light of the questions raised above, this paper examines three issues: managing the body, survival at home, and the nature of everyday life.

MANAGING THE BODY IN EVERYDAY LIFE

Bodily management is an integral part of our everyday lives. This means more of course than body maintenance. As Mellor and Shilling say: 'The flow of daily life is marked by numerous interactions with others in which the body is managed in particular ways, seeks to give off various impressions, and must sometimes "repair" moments of embarrassment' (1997: 21). There is a great deal more to managing the body than carrying out the basic body maintenance activities of the ADLs and IADLs. But our studies found – as have others – that some older people do spend a lot of time on body maintenance (of both kinds). For example, this is how Mr G, an 82-year-old man, with a wife aged 86 who has dementia, describes their typical day[1]:

> A typical day is that I get up at eight o'clock in the morning, have me breakfast. I call her about nine. She has her breakfast. I tidy up while she's having her breakfast. She has about quarter of an hour, twenty minutes break after the breakfast. She gets herself ready and then we go out til dinner time. And then we come back for dinner time, have a nice sandwich at dinner time //// might have a little snooze – she has her sandwich and then sometimes a snooze …

The rest of the day is also described, involving food preparation and feeding, as well as dozing and watching television. His use of the present tense indicates that he sees these activities as routine, things that usually happen. But if one wants to know what actually happens rather than merely how people recount their everyday lives (especially when asked, as Mr G was, about a typical day) one needs to look a little deeper. Thus several instances of reality diverging from the usual were found with Mr G. Here are two extracts from fieldnotes:

> Mr G had previously told me that he goes to the park every day at about 1.45, so I asked him why he wasn't there today. He explained that none of his friends were going, and nothing much happens on a Monday.

---

[1] In excerpts from interviews, //// refers to the omission of part of the transcript.

Friday morning; Mr G was observed to be cleaning. He said Friday was his normal cleaning day.

But in a later interview he answered a question as follows:

> Q   You were hoovering when I came last Friday. Do you do that every Friday?
>
> Mr G Well no. Sometimes I do it on a Saturday. It all depends how I feel. Sometimes I don't feel like it …

With these instances it is not so much that the usual is disrupted by occasional inability to manage, but by the involvement of other people or by how one feels. But ability was also sometimes implicated:

> Mr G told me that he cycled everywhere, though not in the last month as he had fallen off his bicycle when a dog ran out, and had broken his wrist.

Thus it is important to remember that people's bodies give up on them occasionally and temporarily, as well as sometimes permanently.

Also implicated is the failure of equipment. Mrs A is a 95-year-old widow living on her own in a rented, terraced house:

> Q   Do you have a hot water supply?
>
> Mrs A Well, yes. But at the moment, the landlord doesn't know, but it's suddenly packed up on me, and I can switch on the light but the water doesn't get hot. There's a little bit of a hitch. I'm going to wait for a fortnight, until the landlord comes, and he'll take over and have it done. Therefore, I'm handicapped for hot water at the moment.

For Mrs A it is not just the hot water supply that disrupts her ability to have a bath, but also her inability to contact the landlord.

Routine sameness may be described, but everyday life seems characterised by frequent departures from it.

The question in the GHS about whether people can do things only 'with difficulty' may be hard to interpret. Whilst it may seem to imply that an act can only be done with accompanying pain, irritation or tiring effort, it could be a mere matter of the length of time involved. Some people spend a very long time doing things which other people do quickly. Should that be described as 'with difficulty'? For example, Mrs A said she was never available (to see visitors) until twelve o'clock, and her neighbour explained that this was because she took a long while to get up, washed and dressed.

The question of 'managing' to do body maintenance rather than just doing it can also clearly be seen to vary from person to person. Thus Mr G – like many other people in our studies – never referred to managing to do things, he just did them (or not, depending on how he felt, etc.). But Mrs A was very concerned to present herself as someone who was 'managing' (probably because she thought there was a possibility that she would be seen as 'not managing'). For example:

| Q | So let me just ask you what improvements you think could be made to help you get around your home better? |
| Mrs A | I don't think any – because when I go down the cellar I go down backwards, I manage. I think I'm very lucky. |

And later:

| Q | Do you have any difficulty with steps or stairs? |
| Mrs A | Well, I find a way – I manage. |

SURVIVAL AND EVERYDAY LIFE

As Maslow would recognise, survival is not just a matter of how people tend to their own body, but on how they defend their bodies against attack. To survive without help, to feel independent, people do not just talk about body maintenance tasks. Sometimes they think beyond the indoor environment. For example, Mrs A again:

| Q | What do you like best about living in this house? |
| Mrs A | Because I'm independent, and it's a house that's known … In all the yards everybody knows me. And I'm so exposed that other people can see people come to my door. |

So, despite the fact that she said she had not been outside the front door for two years, Mrs A seemed very aware of being situated within a social environment that acted in certain ways towards her.

Survival and body maintenance also take people outside their front doors, not just for shopping, but also for exercise and release of stress. Mr G's wife repeated questions and statements every few minutes. He was reported in fieldnotes as follows:

> I asked if they'd go together (to get the paper), and he replied 'If it's for paper and milk I go on my own, it's quicker. Sometimes we go together, to get her out.' Mrs G then got up and left room. Mr G leant towards me and said 'She keeps repeating herself, I *have* to go out sometimes – she forgets things less than 10 minutes later. It's like water off a duck's back to her. A couple of hours out makes all the difference to me.'

We also found, again as is often the case, that where help was received with body maintenance, it was not just given to people who 'weren't managing'. For example, Mr G did not even think of himself as having 'to manage' but nonetheless his daughter was described as coming 'to help' every week. And another woman, Mrs O, was said to have been confined to bed for two years, waited upon on a rota basis by her several sons and daughters, even though one of the daughters said she could very well do much more than she does; and a son reported on how he had found her downstairs in the kitchen making toast one evening. But, it is not just that people who are independent can manage on their own, and that the frail or disabled cannot. None of us can really manage alone; we all use 'normal' services or technical aids, and if the frail or disabled could make more use of such 'normal' assistance they would be less likely to be seen as dependent. For example, one very active man of 85, when asked about whether he had any meals delivered, replied after some thought: 'Well, the milkman comes every day.'

THE NATURE OF EVERYDAY LIFE IN OLD AGE: MOOCHING AND AMBLING THROUGH THE DAY?

Finally, we can consider whether the everyday life of older people is all about tasks and life at home. Although it is clear that the answer is no, and also that there is considerable variation between people, we need to explore this issue in much more depth. Our research only begins to show some of the areas of interest.

The analysis of people's days often provides very tedious data both about time and about activities, data that barely touch on the fundamental questions. Yet, if we asked people more about what they thought about what they did, and how they would feel if they did not do it (or do feel when they cannot do it) we would learn something more interesting about their everyday lives. For example what are the social rules which underlie the times of day when people do things? Will tomorrow's older people see the morning as the time for tasks and the afternoon for leisure or going out, as some of today's older people do? What kind of activities give people a sense of achievement or satisfy other needs than those of mere body maintenance? Which of them is important to their sense of identity? What opportunities are available to older people to cope with any inability to perform ADLs by adopting strategies which may satisfy them in other ways (such as 'selective optimisation with compensation'; Baltes and Carstensen 1996)?

What does watching television – to take a commonly reported activity – actually mean? How is it used? Mrs A described television (and the newspapers) not just as a way of filling time, nor even just as an interest, but it seemed as a source of company and a vital key to survival:

> Mrs A   My world is the television and the newspapers. I would be lost if I didn't have those two.

Mr and Mrs G used television a lot too, and for them it appeared to be important as an activity through which they could demonstrate sharing and closeness:

> After a pause Mr G announced that they had planned to watch a home movie. I told him this was fine and he went and got one off the shelf and put it in the video recorder. The tape was one and a half hours long of their local club's annual Christmas party. Mr and Mrs G were engrossed, both pointing out people to me and to each other. They were affectionate with each other, smiling as they remembered.

Apart from the distinction between using time and filling time (Young and Schuller 1991), what sort of pace is there to everyday life? Does it vary from person to person or time to time? What speeds it up and what slows it down? For very old people in our studies the pace often seemed slow (if indeed that is how we should interpret the words they use):

> I then asked what he normally did when not at the park. Mr G replied 'I just normally mooch around, watch TV or check my fishing gear.'

Or, as he described his wife:

> Dozing. She's always dozing.

Here is Mrs A talking about how she spends her time:

Mrs A	I'm not a gossiper. I just can't be bothered. While you're talking you can be doing can't you?
Q	And what sort of things do you like to be doing?
Mrs A	I used to be always knitting and crocheting and darning, home things.
Q	And can you still do them?
Mrs A	No, and there's no point.
Q	So what sort of things do you do now?
Mrs A	Well, I just amble through the day.

For others, everyday life had a much faster pace. Here, from our study of people aged 85 and over, is a man of 89 talking about his day:

> I don't sleep much – four or five hours sleep and I'm OK. If I go to bed – I've got to do a lot of reading – so I do it there. I don't read fiction and I don't watch television very much. I play the piano, that's my main relaxation, paint pictures, but I don't do a lot of painting now. I just bought the piano. I've always played and I thought if I had a new piano I might like it better and play a bit more, but often I go several days and don't touch it, because I've got – what with the house and my work and everything – it's just a question of time.

For Mrs A, everyday life is confined to the home. For others it is definitely not. The 'rooms you use during the daytime' that are asked about in the GHS, could be anywhere: place of employment, a friend's or relative's house, the social club, the public house. In our study of people aged 85 and over who were living in their own homes, we found a crucial

16

distinction between those who described themselves as entirely independent and those who did not. This was that the former all talked about active outdoor (or out of home) lives. In the study of dementia, Mr and Mrs G also described the importance of outdoors:

Mr G	In the morning she says to me ...
Mrs G	'Where are we going?'
Mr G	'What have we got on today?' I said 'What do you mean?'
Mrs G	'Where are we going today?' I say. I'm up and dressed and ready to go out. I say to him 'Where are we going?'
Mr G	'Where are we going off for the day?' I say 'Wait a minute, I haven't thought out where we're going to today ...'

REFLECTIONS

Notions of time, the body, the rules which influence how days are occupied, all affect the activities of daily living in later life. Surveys do not allow us to see these contexts and, more importantly, they use questions which are grounded in assumptions about later life. Older people can answer the questions probably because they also accept – or are prepared to go along with – these assumptions. But what do the answers reveal about their everyday lives? Undoubtedly the findings are useful at a population level, though we might suggest a few changes to make them more appropriate to the heterogeneous lives of today's people of 65 years and over.

Social changes make it important, not only for surveys like the GHS to reconsider what is normal or usual for older people, but also for social scientists to chart the changes in the ways in which older people actually live their everyday lives. Climbing backwards down cellar steps to bring up coal for the fire – as described by Mrs A – is already history. Tomorrow's older people will demand more of later life, and their everyday lives will be vastly different. We need to know more about how they are lived, so that we can appreciate the kinds of services and facilities they will find acceptable in frail old age, but also so that housing, employment, pensions, entertainment, education, etc. – where they impinge on daily lives – can be tailored to their purpose.

One of the most important questions we can ask is whether older people control their own everyday lives or are controlled by them. The images presented by the survey questionnaire, of people over 65 whose lives are bounded by whether or not they can manage to carry out tasks at home, are powerful (and probably accepted by many of us and them). Can we perhaps, by comparing the richness of people's own realities with the ADLs of the survey analysts, service providers and clinicians, challenge these images and increase the power of older people to take more control over their lives?

This paper is a plea for further investigation. There is no adequate research on the topic; the few examples used here have merely been able to raise and illustrate some of the issues, which now need to be explored in full.

REFERENCES

Askham, J., Briggs, K., Norman, I. and Redfern, S. (1998) *Accomplishing Care at Home for People with Dementia*, King's College London, Report to NHS Executive North Thames.

Baltes, M. and Carstensen, L. (1996) The process of successful ageing, *Ageing and Society* 16: 397–422.

Bridgwood, A. (2000) *People Aged 65 and Over: Results of an Independent Study Carried out on Behalf of the Department of Health as Part of the 1998 General Household Survey*, Office for National Statistics, London.

Kelly-Hayes, M., Jette, A., Wolf, P., D'Agostino, R. and Odell, P. (1992) Functional limitations and disability among elders in the Framingham study, *American Journal of Public Health* 82: 841–845.

Maslow, A. (1987) *Motivation and Personality*, 3rd edition, Harper Collins, New York.

McGee, M., Johnson, A., Kay, D. *et al.* (1998) The description of activities of daily living in five centres in England and Wales, *Age and Ageing* 27: 605–613.

Mellor, P. and Shilling, C. (1997) *Re-forming the Body: Religion, Community and Modernity*, Sage, London.

Tinker, A., Askham, J., Hancock, R., Mueller, G. and Stuchbury, R. (2000) *Eighty-five Not Out: A Study of People aged 85 and Over at Home*, Anchor Trust, Oxford.

Young, M. and Schuller, T. (1991) *Life after Work: the Arrival of the Ageless Society*, Harper Collins, London.

3

A DAY IN THE LIFE: INTERPRETING FIRST HAND ACCOUNTS FROM THE MASS-OBSERVATION ARCHIVE

DOROTHY SHERIDAN AND CAROLINE HOLLAND

This paper draws on a rich source of largely unpublished autobiographical material about day-to-day events, personal experience, opinion, and reflection. Since 1981, the Mass-Observation Archive (M-OA) at the University of Sussex has been gathering autobiographical material about everyday life in Britain to complement the material already archived from the original project which dates back to 1937. For researchers concerned with the details of the everyday lives of older people, the M-OA includes a unique collection of personal documents which have been written by interested individuals. Their contributions can be idiosyncratic, funny, poignant, thoughtful, political, honest, muddled, revealing. This paper describes something of the origins of this new M-O project, and outlines how the writings are gathered and where they stand in the array of resources available to people studying everyday life.

HISTORICAL BACKGROUND TO MASS-OBSERVATION

The British social research organisation, Mass-Observation, was set up at the end of the 1930s by a group of young upper-class friends based in London. They aimed to create 'an anthropology of ourselves'.[1] From the start, and emerging from an interest in poetry and literature as much as from anthropology, the Mass-Observers encouraged the written recording of everyday life by 'ordinary' people, or what M-O called the 'man and woman in the street'. Between 1937 and 1938, a small panel of volunteers kept a one-day diary for the twelfth day of each month. When World War II began, these one-day diaries became daily diaries. During 1939–45, five hundred people at some time or other wrote full diaries, which they sent

---

[1] A fuller history of the early Mass-Observation can be read in *Mass-Observation: A Short History* Jeffery (1999). For accounts of the contemporary project, see Sheridan (1996) and Sheridan *et al.* (2000).
See also the M-OA website, http://www.sussex.ac.uk/library/massobs

in monthly instalments to M-O's headquarters in London. Some of them continued after the war.

One of the diarists, a woman called Nella Last, began her very detailed and candid diary in 1937 when she was in her late forties and carried on writing until her death in the mid-1960s. This was long after she would have received any encouragement from the M-O organisers, and certainly long after M-O had given up using the diaries as a resource for research. Nella Last's diaries have since been published in an edited form (Broad and Fleming 1981).

In addition to the diarists, a larger group of people, also part of what M-O called its 'national panel', responded to open-ended questions known as *directives* which invited them to describe their lives thematically. They were asked to respond to questions like: What is the food situation like in your area? How do you feel about the Germans? How has war affected your outlook on life? Or, in late 1941, How do you feel about 1942? The responses consist of a mixture of opinion and experience, an amalgam of reporting, observation, self-disclosure, reflection, and analysis. These replies, together with the early diaries, now provide a fruitful resource for the study of the ageing experience of the generations growing older in the years between the late 1930s and the early 1950s.

THE CONTEMPORARY MASS-OBSERVATION PROJECT

It was this element of the original M-O approach which inspired a revival of the national panel in 1981, at a time when biographical methods were out of favour in social research. The inception of the new phase of M-O began as an experiment to see whether people in the early 1980s could be induced to write in the same way as the volunteer diarists and directive respondents of the 1930s and 1940s. As in the early days, Mass-Observers were recruited mainly through letters and articles in newspapers and appeals on the radio. Three hundred recruits by the end of 1981 became twelve hundred by the late 1980s but, since then, the size of the project has been reduced to concentrate on improving the diversity of the panel's composition. The present panel includes around three hundred and fifty people. Over 2800 people have taken part at some time or other, many of them writing over a period of years, or stopping temporarily and then returning.

Three times a year (spring, summer and autumn), the Mass-Observers receive a directive which usually includes two or three different themes. For example, the autumn 2000 directive asked for accounts of family life, in particular the role of gay family members;[2] and also for reactions to various current events and issues in the news. The summer 2000 directive, 'Coming to Britain', was concerned with opinions and personal experiences about economic migrants and political asylum seekers.

A few unsolicited full diaries are received, but they are no longer specifically requested. Instead there are occasional calls for either a detailed one-day diary or a request to keep a continuous diary over a period of time. Such a diary was requested in the autumn 1999 directive to record the beginning of the new millennium. Mass-Observers were asked to keep a two-week diary for the end of the year 1999 and the beginning of the year 2000.

The themes of the directives are intended to be worded as inclusively as possible, and to offer enough variety so that almost everyone on the mailing list feels they can say something. In some cases, differently worded directives are sent to men and women. This approach was chosen when the theme of the directive was menstruation (spring 1996). There are no deadlines and relatively little guidance apart from the discursive and moderately self-disclosing prompts written by Dorothy Sheridan, as director of the project.

Who writes for the project? M-O attracts more men than women; and more white-collar (or middle to lower middle class) recruits than working class recruits. There are only a few writers with Asian or Afro-Caribbean backgrounds. As a writing project, it reflects the nature of writing practices in this society, and it is clear that unless writing for M-O can be understood as congruent with their other writing practices, people are unlikely to feel that they are the 'right' sort of person to volunteer. You need to enjoy writing, and have an interest or belief in the value and meaning of history (Sheridan *et al.* 2000).

---

[2] This directive was a collaborative effort between Dorothy Sheridan and Dr Derek McGee of Southampton University. From time to time, academic researchers commission the M-O Archive to collect material on the theme of their research. New ideas for directive themes are always welcome. The Archive charges for this service since the survival of the whole project depends upon income from external sources.

The Archive is especially rich in accounts by older people, and the project particularly attracts and retains people aged over 50. Of the 367 people on the mailing list at the time of writing, 236 (64 per cent) are aged over 50, 48 per cent are over 60, 33 per cent over 70 and 9 per cent over 80. For gerontologists, this weighting towards the later part of life can be regarded as a strength of the data rather than as a weakness. But, of course, the ages of the respondents are not fixed and, because of the longitudinal nature of participation, many of the people have been writing for several years. They have written about many aspects of their personal lives as well as other events and the subjects of the directives. Whatever their age at the outset they have aged while involved with the Project.

One such correspondent is Bob (Mass-Observer number R470[3]) who joined M-O when it was re-launched in 1981. He was then 47, had been an HGV driver for many years, was married with three children, and lived in a council house in Essex. 'Re your letter in Friday's Mirror' he wrote, 'I would like to take part in your survey'. Bob's interests were 'reading, writing, radio, home brewing, unwilling DIY car mechanics, growing cacti and succulents and general household maintenance'. An officer in the TGWU for 22 years, Bob was an active member of his Tenants' Association and an inactive member of the Labour Party.

Bob has written regularly ever since he joined, not only in response to the directives but also sending in extra essays: 'Once I get a pen in my hand I don't know when to stop', he wrote in 1983. Having written for years with pen and paper, Bob acquired a computer about three years ago and now communicates with the Archive by electronic mail on a very regular basis. He also visits in person from time to time. His approach to writing for M-O is to make his contributions as accessible as possible. In 1983 he wrote:

> Anything I write for you is open to all complete with by-line. There is nothing I have said or done that is so dark a secret that someone somewhere does not know about it. If I give an opinion, that is it, offend or please. I can think of nothing about me which would cause me any concern if it was published on the front page of the Daily Mirror.

---

[3] Normally all the volunteer writers are allocated a number to protect their privacy. Their identities are known to the Archive staff but are disguised on material made available to researchers. This is the preferred arrangements for most participants. However, in this case, Bob has waived his anonymity and given us permission to include the section about him including extracts from his writing under his real name.

This then leads him into a discourse on the British obsession with secrecy.

Bob has written about many of the significant events and processes in his life: on being made redundant; on being a grandfather; on his wife's death after a long illness, and the loss he feels; on his rediscovery of his sexuality at the age of 71. He has written about Labour getting into power in 1997, about his education life story, and about why he writes. He has written about his own ageing.

We have claimed earlier that the M-O Archive contains a wealth of material by and about the experience of ageing. What is especially valuable about the material is that it is also itself a record of the ageing process over 20 years. Taken together, the long-term contributions of Bob and many others means that the M-O Archive provides access to a huge amount of information about the life span. Four people who are now aged over 80 have taken part throughout the 20 years the project has been operating, and fourteen have been writing continuously for more than 15 years; thus recording in considerable detail their thoughts and experiences as they grow older.

Of people who continued to write until their deaths (the relatives of 68 people wrote to tell the Project about their deaths) most were over 70 when they died, and several of them had been born in the nineteenth century. On rare occasions people have decided to resign from the Project because of increasing age. If writing has become physically too hard, people have been encouraged to speak into a tape recorder instead of writing. If a writer feels that they have simply become too old and their world too narrow to continue, they are encouraged to carry on – and are usually pleased to be persuaded.

OLDER PEOPLE AND WRITING

The meaning and value of story telling in later life, and especially of the importance for older people of the processes of autobiographical activity and life review, both oral and written, is well documented. A number of researchers (for example, Coleman 1986; McAdams 1993; Phillipson 1998) have commented on the value of such activities. Describing story telling as one of the most enduring themes of later life, Bornat *et al.* have claimed that:

The social function of the narrative act is ... detected in studies of narration among elderly people living in residential care, in which the life story, as told, may be a product of the social context in which someone lives, a version of a life made ready for public consumption in a situation where identity is at risk from the negative stereotypes of frailty and the processes and procedures of caring. (Bornat *et al*. 2000: 10)

The enjoyment of participating in life review, autobiographical projects and life story competitions by older people has been reported by researchers elsewhere in Europe, Australasia and the Americas, and especially in Scandinavia and Finland where life story projects are especially popular. This reflects the experience of reminiscence and oral history practitioners in Britain and is also consistent with the patterns of participation in the M-O Project.

The predilection of older people to find autobiographical activities rewarding presents us with an extraordinary degree of access to subjective accounts of the ageing experience. The writing provides an opportunity for understanding people's accounts of their experiences as they wish to represent them and as they live through them. Indeed, the very act of research, the making sense of what is told, or claiming significance from it, by another person, underlines the value of these stories and therefore validates the process of recording and writing. While Butler (1963) conceived of the life review as a naturally occurring phenomenon of later life, Brandon Wallace has positioned expressed life stories as occurring in response to a situational challenge, i.e. the request for an account:

From this perspective, older people's talk of the past is seen as a social activity, growing out of and shaped by narrative challenges posed in the course of interaction. (Brandon Wallace 1992: 121)

Brandon Wallace's social constructionist model implies some people will be presented with more narrative challenges than others. Nevertheless some people more than others may be inclined to create or take up opportunities for a narrative exchange, in whatever social encounters they experience – and this reflects Coleman's (1994) distinction between people who choose to reminisce and those who avoid it. The people who have chosen to write for the M-O Project have in general chosen to accept the narrative challenges of the directives – which may take them into territories of reminiscence, self-reflection, and analysis of their own situation and that of the world in general.

They also reflect upon the process of writing itself. Interpretation and analysis become an integral part of the original endeavour of contributing to the M-O Project. The writers write in order to make a contribution to human understanding – not that they actually put it quite like that. Theory-making is not restricted to academics who may be involved in commissioning or using M-OA material: the story telling can itself be theorised by the writers in the process of writing. The writers become *participants in* research rather than *subjects of* research.

An ESRC-funded research project (Street and Sheridan 1994) explored, through both directive replies and interviews with the writers, their motivations for taking part in the M-O Project. A number of reasons were given (or inferred):

- enjoyment of the reading and writing itself

- practice for other writing, or generating 'source material' for other writing

- a reason/structure to organise or develop their thinking: 'sorting out their ideas'

- refreshing their memories about the past, or 'keeping the mind active' (mentioned frequently by older people)

- communicating with other people (some send copies to friends, or let their families read their replies)

- creating space and privacy for themselves for a legitimate goal (often mentioned by women who might not feel able to take time and space for themselves if it was not for a 'research project')

- linking up and identifying with educational activities and ideas

- adding to their own status and sense of self-esteem

- creating an emotional outlet, or for therapeutic or confessional purposes

- finding a safe outlet for political or social views which they felt could not be expressed in their immediate life (NB: participation in the Project is anonymous)

- ensuring that their ideas, thoughts and experience would live after their death. They speak of writing for posterity, for the future, for their grandchildren, or for people like them in future generations.

As one M-O contributor put it:

> When I die, I want to leave things. I don't want to just pop my clogs and they'll say, well, there she goes, cheerio, goodbye. I want them to say, well she wrote a book, she did this writing for Mass-Observation, she knitted me a lovely bedspread, things like that you know. I won't be able to leave any cooking behind will I? I can't leave a cake for posterity! But you know, I'd like to think that there's going to be a lot left of me *really*. (F1373, female in late fifties, interview transcript 1993, p. 19)

The nature of the writing, at intervals throughout the years, makes the resulting document rather different from a life review, or the traditional autobiography which has tended to be more the preserve of older male writers. Langenhove and Harré argue against the monolithic idea of 'one life' told through the traditional vehicle of a literary model of autobiography: 'Life span research cannot thus simply take for granted the so widely spread idea in our western culture that we all have one "biography"' (Langenhove and Harré 1993: 97). For research purposes, they see this autobiographical template as reified, and commend instead what they call 'biographical talk', or orality, which enables people to create re-descriptions of their lives.

Giddens (1991) has argued that the capacity to sustain a narrative supports an individual's identity. People need to create a personal biography which, if an individual is to maintain social relations, is not wholly fictive, and which continually integrates events occurring in the external world. Indeed McAdams (1993) suggests that the life story *is* identity: in a continual process of making and re-making, the life story or personal myth is shaped both by new events and by the evaluations of those events which contribute to future revisions of the story. Identity is conferred through the construction of a coherent and credible narrative.

The capacity to describe and re-describe is not a discursive practice limited to oral communication, but it is apparent within the writings of the Mass-Observers. Over many years they may re-invent themselves and their biographies, telling the same stories from different angles depending on the theme of the directive; or different stories at different stages of their life. Mass-Observers might contest McAdam's interpretation of what it is that they do; but many of them would acknowledge the benefits to themselves of being able to re-visit and re-interpret aspects of their lives.

USING THE M-O ARCHIVE MATERIAL FOR RESEARCH ON AGEING

M-O material is not representative in the sense of being statistically generalisable to the whole population, and thus it cannot be understood in the same way as material generated as part of a sample survey. It would be better described as a correspondence or dialogue which generates material more usefully analysed using qualitative methodologies.

The M-O Archive comprises an enormous collection of data on older people's lives written over the last twenty years of the twentieth century, some of it about the here and now, much of it recollecting the past, mixing together as the themes suggest or according to temperament and experience. What unites this collection is that it comes from the point of view of the writers themselves. These documents are constructed narratives: and this raises interesting issues about the discourses of everyday life, and the modes of communication which people select from a culturally determined repertoire in order to take part in the M-O Project. Indeed there is some evidence of a M-O 'genre' emerging, which draws on the family letter, the school essay, the newspaper report, the personal diary, the testimony, the confessional, and so on – as the writers feel inclined.

Two extracts from a 1992 directive are presented here to illustrate the flexibility of the M-O genre. The directive asked people to write about personal hygiene: specifically about certain items such as soap, toilet paper, toothpaste, etc.; and more generally about attitudes to hygiene now and in the past. In the first extract, the correspondent describes how she has used the directive as a prompt to think about the origins of her present-day habits and predilections. Relating a personal story, she nevertheless includes elements of a social history which many other people from a similar background would recognise. She writes fluently as she vividly recalls the past, in a style which is more crafted than one would expect for example in a transcription from an interview, but in a style which retains its immediacy.

Friends and relations know I will always appreciate good soap as a gift. If I go into a shop where damaged or other boxes are on sale I always buy some ... whether I want it or not. I have often asked myself why? I rarely use perfume so I felt it must have a buried reason. Thinking about this 'Observation' I have gone back to my childhood days and found the answer. As a child I lived in a tiny house ... no bathroom or tapped hot water. Bath night was a Friday when the old tin bath was taken off the wall, placed in front of the kitchen hob, where lots of kettles were heating water. It was a case of youngest first, then the next until all had had their bath! But it was the soap, a long bar of either carbolic or household soap, an old kitchen knife was used to cut 'slices' off and the smell was perfectly horrible.

When I was about 7 or 8 I was sent into the country to be cared for whilst my mother was ill. It was a little village with a small village store. I can remember so clearly going in to spend my Saturday Penny and seeing on the counter small bars of lavender soap and I think it was manufactured by Grossmiths'. The beautiful fragrance fascinated me and whilst waiting to be served I used to sniff the little bars. I asked how much it was but my penny was not enough to buy one. On the last Saturday I was there I told the owner I was going home. Then, she said "well here is a little gift for you to take with you, I've watched you sniffing". Oh what a thrill I had vowed to keep it for ever and ever but shortly after we moved and had a bathroom and I did use the soap. That stemmed off my love for soap it is quite evident. I can remember also an advertisement I think it was Erasmus for Miss Violet and Blanche Lovely mauve and white soap. I cannot recall the fragrance of the white, but the mauve was violet. So I am in the habit of using expensive soap, I live alone and apart from an occasional visitor I use it all myself. (B 36: female aged 77 years)

In the second extract from the same directive, the respondent uses the directive to talk about her perceptions of personal hygiene problems for pensioners, and her anxieties about dealing with her own ageing. She also gives an account of how her life has changed as she has aged, resulting in different routines and priorities. In accounting for this, she also reveals some of the anxieties of living on a restricted income – perhaps an unexpected outcome from a question about personal hygiene, but typical of the flexibility and creativity in M-O responses.

> And I must remember, as I get older, that some old pensioners do forget to wash, or can't afford to heat bathwater, or think it doesn't matter. Their kitchens get dirty, and their bed linen gets grubby, so I suppose they don't notice. But I must keep it up. I also have a sneaking suspicion my daughters keep an eye on me! Is Mum getting old and forgetful? She has her 'little ways', they're clearly thinking to themselves, as their sharp hawk-like eyes take in some of my muddles which I am going to clear up, but I've got to do this or that first. I'm not that old yet, I'm only 65, and as fit & active as they are, but I suppose they're getting ready for my first fall from grace. They are watchful! Alzheimers' waits.
>
> I find I no longer need a deodorant. I live a gentler life than I did. I don't get into an emotional stew at work, and I don't play games or get very hot, and my "roller" deodorant has mostly dried up. Soap and water copes with my daily dirt. – But heating up a tankful of hot water for a bath is expensive. My electricity bill is already something I dread each quarter, as it takes all the money in my Bank to pay it that particular month. I've managed to space out other big bills like insurance, car tax, telephone so that I can make it financially, but even so I've decided to have a bath every other day, to make it easier. (B1950: female aged 65 years)

These two responses give a small indication of the variability and complexity of the information which researchers can expect from M-O directives on *specific themes*.

M-O *diaries* present another form of data. They are also concerned with both the day-to-day activities of the diarists and the 'external' events of the time in which they were written, but they can be more formally constructed than responses to themed directives. The diaries contain a whole range of information about the nitty-gritty of the everyday life of the writers – but they can also contain lyrical descriptions of life in the county or the town; discussions of contemporaneous political and social issues; or reflections of family relationships. They reflect what the writers thought was significant or of interest in accounting for their day. For the researcher, the interest of these diaries lies primarily in their ability to capture the writer's experience of the everyday with its complex mixture of the mundane and the exceptional, the personal and the public:

> Personal journals are particularly suitable sources of information about what it is like to be an older person; in them the authors attempt to fixate the meaning of the day-to-day flow of experience. They are effective at capturing changes of mood and the subjectivity of the moment, but they also go beyond the moment and embed the flux of experience in larger contexts of meaning. (Berman 1994: 212)

The two extracts below relate to Friday, 13 March 1992, in response to a call for a one-day diary. The first appears to have been written retrospectively and rather reflectively, and it was preceded by a page about the context (the fact that the diarist's son was staying; a General Election had been called; the possible closure of the local bank).

> ... Spring is going on – small lambs in the fields all around us, wild birds feeding from my table, my own hens laying, days getting longer, crocuses, pansies, polyanthus coming out, and my first tulips too. I saw a rook carrying a stick for nest-building.
>
> 6.30 a.m. I woke up, it isn't light enough yet. Oh hell, I've got a headache. This is misery.
>
> 6.45 a.m. I got up, pulled on my dressing gown, gumboots in the kitchen, pick up seed & pellets & stagger out to the hens. Its grey, windy, cold, trying to rain. I let out the five hens and the Cocky Griff and his six wives. He ignores the grain & immediately hares after Hetty, his ruff out, wings half out, long legs ... and pounces on her. Then he rushes off after Custard, or Flo, & he "does" her. Then he eats. Wild birds come through the bushes. My hens are free range and give lovely eggs. I go back to bed and warm up. Go to sleep.
>
> 9 a.m. I get up, dress etc, and [for headache I took a paracetamol] have bacon and tomato for breakfast toast and half grapefruit. I woke [son] up, but he only rolled over. The radio was Desert Island Disks, Sue Lawley's guest was Jocelyn Stevens who was a journalist but had been to Eton and was very high class. I washed up, tidied kitchen.
>
> (B1950; female, 65 years, 'living in small cottage in Anglesey')

The second extract in contrast appears to have been written in real time. This captures the diarist's anxiety about whether or not to travel to Somerset, but is less reflective on the day in context:

> Having slept well I enjoyed 5.45-7.00 a.m. in lounge & kitchen. I spun-dry trousers & tights, for drying on bathroom radiator, ironed shirts, etc., cooked some fruit. Listened to Weather Forecast. We are hoping to stay in Somerset Mon 16 – Fri 20 & will be phoning the friend we're to stay with, at 6.0 pm. We don't have a car. Heard incidental radio jems. Prayed for those living on this Mobile Home Site & for wisdom re. Our Somerset visit.
>
> 8.0 a.m. breakfast in the lounge Tea, porridge with the stewed fruit, brown bread & marmalade. Washed up. Stayed till 8.30 to hear S.E. news on T/V.
>
> Then To bedroom till 10.30. It's now 9.0 so I'll air bed & be ready for the repeat of Desert Island Disks. It's Jocelyn Stevens – I've never heard of him – worth giving my whole attention to – get airing done on 3 radiators ...
>
> ... T/V 5.40-7.30 & will have phoned Taunton before I write again.
>
> 7.30 We'd heard weather forecast for snow coming South and our friend understood it might not be weather for us to travel to Somerset. Will phone her again tomorrow. Disappointing for all but, as we've cancelled milk, etc., we may make last minute plans to stay locally.
>
> (C2147 female, 70 years, 'retired infant teacher')

The brief extracts presented here give some of the flavour of intimacy and disclosure with which the Mass-Observers approach their chosen task. Taking part in the project enables people, who might not otherwise have the impetus or the opportunity, to write themselves into the historical record. The combination of longitudinal and biographical data is exceptional and lends itself to many forms of theoretical approaches. Once gathered, it can be 'mined' indefinitely from many different angles. The material itself is rich and varied. It will often raise more questions than it answers, and in this respect it can be an invaluable source of inspiration for further research.

REFERENCES

Berman, H.J. (1994) Analyzing personal journals of later life, in Gubrium, J. and Sankar, A. (eds) *Qualitative Methods in Aging Research,* Sage, Thousand Oaks, CA.

Bornat J. *et al.* (eds) (2000) *Oral History Health and Welfare*, Routledge, London.

Brandon Wallace, J. (1992) Reconsidering the life review: The social construction of talk about the past, *The Gerontologist* 32(1):120–125.

Broad, R. and Fleming, S. (eds) (1981) *Nella Last's War*, Falling Wall Press, Bristol.

Butler, R. (1963) The life review: An interpretation of reminiscence in the aged, *Psychiatry* 26: 65–75.

Coleman, P. (1986) *Ageing and Reminiscence Processes: Social and Clinical Implications*, John Wiley and Sons, Chichester.

Giddens, A. (1991) *Modernity and Self-identity: Self and Society in the Late Modern Age,* Polity Press, Cambridge.

Jeffery, T. (1999) *Mass-Observation: A Short History*, Mass-Observation Archive Occasional Paper No. 10, University of Sussex Library, Brighton.

Langenhove, L. and Harré, R. (1993) Positioning and autobiography: telling your life, in Coupland, N. and Nussbaum, J. (eds) *Discourse and Life Span Identity*, Sage, Thousand Oaks, CA

McAdams, D.P. (1993) *The Stories We Live By: Personal Myths and the Making of the Self,* Morrow, New York.

Phillipson, C. (1998) *Reconstructing Old Age: New Agendas in Social Theory and Practice*, Sage Publications, London.

Sheridan, D. (1996) *Damned Anecdotes and Dangerous Confabulation: Mass-Observation as Life History*, Mass-Observation Archive Occasional Paper No 10, University of Sussex Library, Brighton.

Sheridan, D., Street, B. and Bloome, D. (2000) *Writing Ourselves: The Mass-Observation Project and Literary Practices,* Hampton Press, Creskill, NJ.

Street, B. and Sheridan, D. (1994) *Literacy Practices and the Mass-Observation Project*, ESRC End of Project Report, R000233728.

4

EVERY DAY'S THE SAME? A STUDY OF THE MANAGEMENT OF LONG-TERM MEDICATION

BILL BYTHEWAY AND JULIA JOHNSON

INTRODUCTION

Empirical research on 'everyday living' has to focus on what happens *in reality*, day by day. It requires samples of days lived, not just samples of people to interview. For many purposes, it is not good enough to assume that how people describe their everyday lives is an adequate representation of the reality of those lives. The challenge that empirical researchers face is how to obtain, interpret and analyse data specifically about *events* and *actions* that occur in the course of everyday life.

In this paper we draw upon research that concerns one specific aspect of the everyday lives of older people – the management of long-term medication. In planning a study, funded by the Department of Health, of how this is accomplished by people aged 75 or more, we wanted to obtain systematic data about the routine and non-routine consumption of medicines. Ideally we wanted to observe what actually happens but this, of course, is impossible in the privacy of a person's own home, particularly when it involves bedroom and bathroom as well as kitchen. Even should observation be possible, we could not be certain that we would be observing what would have happened had we not been there.

We knew, however, that some people with long-term illnesses do keep logs of medication and symptoms to help the doctor diagnose and monitor treatment. So we decided that, potentially, there was much to be gained by asking research subjects to keep a diary for a short period of time.

We reviewed some literature on the use of diaries and noted, for example, Ken Plummer's conclusion in 1983 that 'there still remains remarkably little sociological usage [of diaries]' (1983: 18). Despite this, he was able to contrast three broad strategies in using commissioned diaries, and we were attracted to the diary/interview method (1983: 19–20). In particular we were persuaded by the argument of Zimmerman and Wieder that:

By requesting that subjects keep a chronologically organized diary or log of daily activities, we in effect asked for a record of their own performances ... Completed diaries functioned for us in a way similar to the field notes turned in by our regular research assistants. Diarists thus served as adjunct ethnographers of their own circumstances. (Zimmerman and Wieder 1975: 484)

They argued that the interview that followed, based upon the diary, was crucial. The diary, combined with the information resulting from the interview,

affords at least the possibility of gaining *some degree of access to naturally occurring sequences of activity*, as well as raising pertinent questions about their meaning and significance. (Zimmerman and Wieder 1975: 485; emphasis added)

To us, this suggested that the *interview* in which the subject amplifies upon a *diary* that they *themselves* have kept, has the potential to generate revealing empirical material concerning events that make up everyday life. Whatever the problems in interpreting the data, it would, at the very least, offer a perspective on medication that would differ from that obtained solely by interviewing.

THE DEVELOPMENT OF THE DIARY

For our study, we obtained what we consider a 'good representative sample' of 77 people aged 75 or over registered with eight practices in contrasting parts of England and Wales. Those who had not been taking prescribed medication for twelve months or more, and those who were in long-term residential, nursing or hospital care, were excluded. We have described elsewhere the procedure we adopted for sampling and gaining the agreement of participants (Bytheway *et al.* 2000).

The information leaflet that we produced and gave to every prospective participant explained in detail the purpose of the research and how it would be conducted: being interviewed several times by a fieldworker, showing the fieldworker their medicines and how they were stored, keeping a fourteen-day diary, and agreeing to the research team having access to his or her medical records. In the leaflet we indicated that participants were free to decline any of our requests and to drop out at any point.

The following instructions were included on the front page of the diary. They indicate how we endeavoured to create a diary-keeping routine and how we planned to make use of the diary in structuring the interviews:

> Think of this as an ordinary diary. There are fourteen pages, one page for each day of the fortnight. We have divided the day up into hours, and we have given you boxes to tick and a space at the top and bottom for you to make notes.
>
> According to the time, we want you to tick a box whenever:
>
> 1. you take your medicines
>
> 2. you feel symptoms or pains
>
> 3. you have a meal or snack
>
> 4. you have or make a phone call
>
> 5. visitors call
>
> 6. you go out visiting or shopping
>
> When we come back to check the diary, we would like to ask you about these things. We are specially interested in when you take your medicines and whether anything out of the ordinary upsets your routines.
>
> So *whenever you tick a box, make a note* of what the symptom was, what medicines you took, who visited you, or whatever. Just enough to help you remember.
>
> Try to fill the diary in whenever it's convenient. At some point each morning, you should think back over the previous twelve hours and check that the diary is up-to-date. Likewise you should do the same in the evening.
>
> We hope you find this an interesting – or even helpful – exercise. We will keep in touch with you during the fortnight and will come to collect the diary when it is over. Many thanks for your help.

In designing the diary, we decided that it should cover two weeks: anything longer might be too demanding for the participant, and unmanageable for later analysis. Anything shorter would not guarantee us at least one uninterrupted and full week of diary entries. Each of the fourteen days is represented by a double-page spread which includes a

6x24 grid. Each of the 24 columns represents one hour and each double page the 24 hour day.

In deciding which aspects of daily life to include, we wanted to set medication into a broader context and so we reasoned as follows: first, there is the consumption of medication itself and this is typically closely associated with both the experience of symptoms and the consumption of meals. Secondly, it is frequently the case that social contacts and activities – specifically, phone calls, visitors, visits and shopping – affect and are affected by symptoms, meals and medication, and they may be involved in the business of renewing supplies of medicines.

In specifying these six aspects, we created a structure for the diarists which, we hoped, would assist them in producing a record of how medication fitted into their daily lives. The grid occupied the middle third of each spread; the remainder was left blank for diarists to enter notes and other pertinent information.

We piloted the diary with six patients. This led to a number of minor improvements in the design of the diary. More significantly we realised that the above instructions, written on the first page of the diary, were not easy to absorb and that some participants needed help in getting the diary started. We employed seven fieldworkers for the main study; all had experience of social science fieldwork but none had any professional training in health care. It was important that they used an effective and standardised strategy in relation to the completion of the diary. The following was how they recruited and assisted the diarists.

The practice nurse in each of eight practices passed on to us the names and addresses of ten eligible patients who had agreed to participate. In the first interview with the participant, the fieldworker explained that, although we would like them to complete the diary themselves, this was not essential. If they wished, they could have the help of 'a scribe'. In addition, they were free to refuse to keep a diary whilst agreeing to an interview.

The outcome of this initial negotiation is that three of the 77 refused a diary being kept by anyone, 10 agreed to a scribe (in three instances, this was the fieldworker), and 64 participants agreed to being the diarist themselves.

The participant or scribe was then given the diary and shown how to complete it. Through our pilot study we had found that the most effective way of doing this was for the fieldworker to say 'Let's go back to this time yesterday' and then, with the participant (and diarist), to begin making appropriate entries for the 24 hours that followed. In this way, most of the entries for Days 1 and 2 were made by the fieldworker. This was done with the participant providing information and the fieldworker showing how entries could be made. The fieldworker checked that the participant understood the grid and suggested ways of making notes that the participant could sustain. Thus, in most instances, Day 3 was the first day in the diary to be filled in solely by the participant. It was interesting to note from the tapes of these interviews that many of the participants, and occasionally the fieldworker, slipped into the historic present ('And what do you do then?' 'Well, I always make sure that I ...') rather than the past tense ('And what did you do then?' 'Well, last night I made sure that I ...'). This in itself demonstrates not only the power of routine but also the pervasive assumption that our research was intended to document the usual rather than the actual.

At some point during the next interview, a few days later, the fieldworker looked over the diary to see how it was progressing and may have made notes in it about actions the participant had not recorded. In six instances the fieldworker found that the participant had not made any entries. Where possible, and similarly in other instances where the participant was having difficulty, the fieldworker would again use the procedure of going back over the previous 24 hours.

On the final visit, prior to the diary being handed over, the fieldworker made sure it was completed as fully as possible. Nine of the participants had stopped making entries before the 14th day and of these six had made entries on less than seven days. Put another way, of the 77, 47 participants handed over a diary that had entries on every one of the 14 days.

THE EVALUATION

We have undertaken an evaluation of this method (Bytheway and Johnson 2001). Here we present a summary of our conclusions. For the evaluation, we considered five questions:

- *Representativeness:* to what extent does such a demanding research tool put potential participants off, creating a sample that is more biased than would otherwise have been the case? We concluded that the request did put off between 5 per cent and 10 per cent of those approached and that this did create some additional, but relatively minor, biases in our sample.

- *Difficulties:* were some participants unable to complete the diary due to visual impairment, problems of manual dexterity or limited literacy skills? We found that it had caused some difficulties for a few participants but the option of a scribe had been an effective way of coping with this. Also the structure of the grid made it relatively easy for diarists to tick boxes and make notes, without the anxieties (that might have come with a less structured diary) of 'what was I supposed to enter?'

- *Quality of data:* how consistent, adequate and accurate was the diary as a record of daily events and actions? We found that there was a significant decline over the first week in the average number of words entered. There was no further decline over the course of the second week, however, and so we concluded that there was an initial tendency to embellish early entries with supplementary detail. For 38 of the completed diaries, the fieldworker made entries on days other than the first two and this indicates that they had judged some diary pages to be inadequate. In almost every case, however, these were additional notes rather than ticked boxes. There was some evidence that, in a few cases, entries reflected standard routines rather than actual events. More significantly, perhaps, we concluded that almost certainly many acts of medication were not recorded, particularly those involving creams and ointments or non-prescribed medicines. In part this was because the participants did not consider them to be medicines and in part because we had instructed the fieldworkers to give priority to medicines being prescribed on a repeat basis.

- *Influencing behaviour:* did keeping a diary influence behaviour? We realised that at a simple level the diary was a form of reminder and, as such, behaviour was bound to be influenced. There was no direct evidence of this but some entries did suggest that keeping the diary might have raised consciousness in the participants regarding their medication.

- *Ethical considerations:* does the completion of a diary, and all that goes with it, cause undue distress, anxiety or inconvenience? The project did raise certain ethical issues and one person in particular was upset by her failure to sustain the diary (for a fuller discussion of this, see Bytheway and Johnson 2001: 199). Although this was very regrettable, it was evident that many others had acted on our assurances that all aspects of participation were optional.

The evaluation focused on the weaknesses of the diary as a research method and, as a result, our confidence in the value of the data it produced was somewhat undermined. There were many ways in which we were left uncertain about what a particular diary told us about what had actually happened. Nevertheless, the evaluation also showed us how much the diaries had revealed about daily routines of medication, and we found it hard to think how else this could have been achieved. So we concluded that the diary did provide us with insights if not hard evidence into what actually happens day by day (Bytheway and Johnson 2002).

EXAMPLE

There is a strong argument, of course, that we should interpret the diary as a *construction* by the participant drawing upon, rather than reflecting, actual events and actions. As such we should be as sceptical about the accounts that it produces as about any other method of data collection, be it interview, observation or questionnaire.

To test this argument, we thought that it would be sensible to work through one particular case study. Miss Neal (a pseudonym) is 86 and lives alone. She has three main health concerns: arthritis, breathlessness due to blood pressure, and poor eyesight. She kept her own diary although the fieldworker added notes on all but two of the 14 days. She needed a lot of encouragement:

> She was quite troubled when I showed her the diary and how to fill it in … She had very poor eyesight and 'wobbly' handwriting, and felt that she would be unable to fill in the diary sufficiently. Much of the first visit was spent reassuring her, and going through the diary again and again until she felt comfortable. In the end, I feel that she did a wonderful job.

She showed the fieldworker her medicines, who listed four repeat prescribed medicines: tablets for her blood pressure and pain due to arthritis, eye drops, and cream for her arthritic back and limbs. On forms that we supplied, the practice nurse, using the practice records, recorded the same four prescribed medicines. Miss Neal also showed six medicines that she had bought in her local pharmacy, primarily creams.

When we turn to the diary, Day 1 was completed by the fieldworker. It is interesting to note here the tendency noted above, to record what 'usually happens': the breakfast is detailed with the bracketed comment 'every morning'; likewise Miss Neal's supper at 9pm. Also there is a note that eye gel is 'put in whenever there is pain'. This was not the kind of note that we had hoped to find in the diary. Despite this, the fieldworker has provided a clear record of the first 24 hours, making it clear that Miss Neal had suffered from *constant* breathlessness. Interestingly, Miss Neal herself entered a note on Day 1 about taking a Co-codamol at 9pm. Perhaps she made this entry the following day when checking over Day 1.

Turning to the early hours of Day 2, there is more information about what happens *every night,* and then there is a note of the visit of the fieldworker at 10am. From here on, most of the entries are made by Miss Neal herself but, at the following interview (on Day 7), the fieldworker added further notes for the preceding days although, interestingly, this time she overlooked recording her own visit. Regarding the value of the interview, it is interesting that there is a line drawn through the row for symptoms on Day 5. This should be set against the following extract from the transcribed interview:

Miss Neal	I, I haven't put any symptoms down you see, er, …
FW	Yeah, I'll just put through here. [drawing the line]
Miss Neal	… because I'm breathless but I didn't put well, all that, that down.
FW	No, because we put that at the beginning didn't we [referring back to the note on Day 1 about constant pain], that you're pretty, well, constantly breathless.
Miss Neal	Yes.

Similarly, the fieldworker checked the tick for medication at 9pm on Day 5 and then commented:

FW	Ah. And on that evening you took a tablet, was that a Co-codamol again?
Miss Neal	Yes. I take two every night.

Again, when she got to Day 7, she checked Miss Neal's breakfast medication:

FW   And then on the Sunday ... Oh, you had an early breakfast that morning, didn't you?

Miss Neal   Yes.

FW   So did you take your er ... blood pressure tablet after breakfast that day? You ticked nine o'clock, you took it after breakfast.

Miss Neal   After breakfast. I always take it after breakfast.

On Day 9 (7th of April), Miss Neal recorded in her diary going to see her doctor. He prescribed her Zestril. This new medicine is recorded as being taken that evening and, at the third interview, it was added by the fieldworker to the Prescribed Medicines log. Also, at that interview, the usual daily and weekly routines were completed by the fieldworker. Miss Neal reports that her usual daily routine includes the eye gel before breakfast (but not the tablets with breakfast) and the tablets with her supper.

There were thirteen participants including Miss Neal who have a fixed twice-a-day routine of medication and she is representative of those whose routine was subjected to some disruption during the course of the fortnight. The following is our summary of what we learned about her pattern of medication. Our sources were her diary, the fieldworker's report and the taped interviews:

In interview, Miss Neal described how she takes her medicines routinely at around 8 or 9 in the morning and again at 9 or 10 in the evening. In between times she goes out most days.

Looking at her diary, we find evidence that routinely she applies drops to her eyes when washing before breakfast. During the first week she then had a blood pressure tablet after breakfast. In the early hours of Day 5, however, she made a note of 'pain in neck and head'. This pain woke her again at 4am on Day 9. She went to see her doctor after breakfast, who changed her medicine and gave her a new prescription of Zestril (lisinopril) for her blood pressure problem. She took her first tablet that evening and continued taking it at the same time over the following days. She had noted on Day 1 that she always has Shredded Wheat, tea and biscuits in the evening, and this had coincided during the first week with her taking Co-codamol as a routine medication to control pain. In the second week, however, this pattern was unsettled and she also began to take Co-codamol during the day. Also twice she took it at night to alleviate pain. Despite this change in her medication, her basic routines were not changed and on Day 12, even though she took the painkiller at 3am in the morning, she went into town at midday to shop and have lunch out.

We designed a diagram (which we called a Medigram) for plotting out the diary record of medication. Miss Neal's Medigram reveals the regularity of medication taken twice a day coupled with the occasional additional treatment of pain. The Medigram also dramatically summarises the impact of the visit to the doctor on Day 9.

This case study demonstrates well how a combined analysis of both diary and interviews reveals a sequence of events which leads to a change in prescribed medication. We were able to check this account against the practice's records and these confirm the prescription of Zestril on 7th April (Day 9) and this was renewed on 26th May.

The fieldworker returned for a third and final interview on 15th April (equivalent to Day 17 of the diary). Here she reviewed the problems Miss Neal had had over Easter (Day 11, 12th April, was Easter Sunday that year):

FW	And it just got very, very bad over Easter?
Miss Neal	It did. Oh dear, I was in pain.
FW	Did you take any more medication for that?
Miss Neal	I I took … er, you see, I can't take arthritis tablets because of [INAUDIBLE]
FW	That's right, yeah.
Miss Neal	And I daren't take too many Co-codamol, but one night I did, I got up at three o'clock in the morning. Sunday.
FW	Oh, you put it in the diary. [Presumably this was Day 12 of the diary]
Miss Neal	I got up at three o'clock. I couldn't rest in bed.

FW	No, that's not doing you any good is it, if you can't …?
Miss Neal	No, though it did get me to sleep. And the doctor's changed it now the blood pressure tablets.
FW	Right.
FW	That's right, I remember, the last visit I made.
Miss Neal	Yes, and er, [INAUDIBLE] so he's changed them twice. And he took them back. [PAUSE] And I put them there.
FW	You're keeping them in the drawer where you used to keep the other ones.
Miss Neal	Yes because I can, at night I put them here. For the first week, he told me to take them every night, and then, and then go on to morning Saturday first week.
FW	Do you know why that was? Why he asked you … Why he thought: take them at night for the first week …?
Miss Neal	I don't know, no I don't know. But I took them. I went on the Tuesday.
FW	Right.
Miss Neal	I started on the Tuesday.
FW	Right. It's so handy having all those, you know the days of the week for each tablet.
Miss Neal	Then I took them, er for a week.
FW	In the evening.
Miss Neal	In the evening. That was Monday night and then I started again on Tuesday this week, Tuesday this week, in the morning.

The Medigram for Miss Neal

Hr	Day 1	2	3	4	5	6	7	8	9	10	11	12	13	14	Total
1															
2															
3												c			1
4									c						1
5															
6															
7															
8		b	b	b	b	b	b	b	b	b	b	b	b	b	13
9	a	a	a	a	a	a	a	a	a			c			10
10					c					c			c		3
11														c	1
12															
13															
14															
15															
16															
17															
18															
19															
20											c				1
21		c	c	c	c	c	c	c	d				d		9
22	c	c							c	d	d	d	c	d	8
23														c	1
24															

KEY

a Amlodopine Besylate 5mg (one daily)

b Viscotears Gel 10g (one drop as necessary)

c Co-codamol 8/500 (two up to four times a day)

d Lisinopril Dihydrate 2.5mg (one daily)

FW	And how are you finding these?
Miss Neal	Well, I'm not as breathless, … I am breathless but I'm not as breathless, as I was.
FW	Ah, are these any stronger, or are they just a different?
Miss Neal	I don't know, I don't know. He's trying me on them. I have to go and see him on Tuesday.
FW	Right.
Miss Neal	And then he's going to take my blood pressure. You see they're blood pressure tablets.
FW	Yeah.
Miss Neal	And he's going to see whether they calm my blood pressure, whether they're working for my blood pressure, you see.

CONCLUSION

In this analysis we have concentrated on medication. The participants' diaries and interviews also provide insights into their changing diets and patterns of social contact. It is possible to spend a long time reading through the transcripts of interviews, checking them against the diaries and logs, and against the records produced by the practice nurses, and slowly but surely gaining an understanding of their daily lives. As in courtroom procedures, it can seem that 'the truth' begins to emerge. It may be more appropriate to refer to it as 'a truth', but in our view the important point is that it is a truth rather than a fiction.

Inevitably of course, the data generate all sorts of questions: about the accuracy and completeness of the records, and about what 'actually happened'. It is possible that the information we obtained from a participant is all a total fabrication. The fieldworker was with the participant for an overall average of three hours which, in the context of fourteen days, is not sufficient to constitute adequate observation. Nevertheless, they were instructed to record what happened while they were there and, in being shown the participant's medicines, they were able to see how they were stored and handled. For the most part, most of the participants displayed, and occasionally expressed, a commitment to producing a record of 'the truth' and we the research team are morally obliged to accept what they have offered us on that basis. Having undertaken the project (even though we ourselves only undertook fieldwork in the pilot phase), we do believe that we have learnt something of the truth about what happened in the course of the forty-seven recorded fortnights for which we have full diaries.

This brings us to our final point and this, we would argue, is crucial to the further development of gerontology. Interviews with people aged 75 or more, in the spoken word recorded on audiotape and transcribed on paper, tend to reflect the familiar image of 'the elderly person': homely, comfortable, passive, tired, friendly, funny, deferential, nostalgic, alienated: the list of adjectives could go on almost indefinitely. Despite the diversity that is often evident within samples and which the researcher might feature, there is a homogenising familiarity about the accounts that arise from the standard interview setting and discourse. As the interviewee struggles to answer questions and say what they hope the interviewer might want to hear, as the interviewer struggles to create opportunities for interviewees to say 'what they think', as gerontologists struggle to articulate what they have learnt about later life from such interviews, and from reading or listening to comparable accounts of other research, it seems possible that what has emerged is a stereotype.

What can be produced through diaries is a different image. Despite their frequent claims to leading an ordinary and routine life in which 'every day is the same', what many of our participants recorded in their diaries was a day-to-day struggle to maintain these routines in the face of a myriad of threats and challenges and, simultaneously, their enterprise in taking advantage of non-routine opportunities.

REFERENCES

Bytheway, B., Johnson, J., Heller, 'I'. and Muston, R. (2000) *The Management of Long-term Medication by Older People*. Report to the Department of Health, School of Health and Social Welfare, The Open University, Milton Keynes.

Bytheway, B. and Johnson, J. (2001) An evaluation of the use of diaries in a study of medication in later life, *International Journal of Social Research Methodology* 4(3): 183–204.

Bytheway, B. and Johnson, J. (2002) Doing diary-based research, in Jamieson, A. and Victor, C.R. (eds) *Researching Ageing and Later Life*, Open University Press, Buckingham.

Plummer, K. (1983) *Documents of Life,* George Allen and Unwin, London.

Zimmerman, D.H. and Wieder, D.L. (1975) The diary-interview method, *Urban Life* 5(4): 479–497.

5

THE USE OF DIARIES TO STUDY THE EVERYDAY FOOD LIFE OF OLDER PEOPLE

ANGELA DICKINSON

INTRODUCTION

Food and eating are a fundamental part of everyday life. Yet at the beginning of the twenty-first century, how much do we know about the context of food and eating and the role they play in the lives of older people?

This paper describes a study in which I set out to explore this aspect of later life. In particular, I analyse and evaluate the use of food diaries as a tool that provides insight into the everyday reality of food use for older people. Also the use of food diaries by nutritionists is briefly examined. Aspects of routine and living together are used to illustrate how I used diaries in this study, and to explore their value as a research tool.

BACKGROUND

Historically, nutrition emerged as a distinct field of study from within biomedicine, a discipline which is grounded within the positivist paradigm and heavily reliant on quantitative research techniques. So there has been a tendency within the nutritional sciences to rely on research evidence of a statistical nature.

The recent extensive study of the nutritional status of older adults is an example of this. Funded jointly by the Department of Health and the Ministry of Agriculture Fisheries and Food (Finch *et al*. 1998), it was the first national study to be undertaken with this age group for over twenty years. While documenting nutritional status as measured by various food intake measures based on a four-day food diary, and by anthropometric and blood analytical measures, it has neglected to describe the associated social and psychological factors which influence food intake. Germov and Williams have challenged the value of this approach for the study of nutrition:

Nutritionists and dietitians have largely been concerned with the 'post-swallowing' studies, but the benefit to public health has been limited since the knowledge is divorced from the social context of its application. (Germov and Williams 1996: 98)

Measures which seek to improve the nutritional status of older people need to be based on an understanding of *why* and *how* foods are chosen; that is, on the non-biological meanings of food. Eating food is an integral part of everyday life and is rarely undertaken purely to satisfy biological need. A study focusing upon the socio-cultural aspects of the dietary habits of older people therefore has the potential to add a further dimension to knowledge.

THE STUDY

The aim of my study was to gain an insight into the processes involved in the construction of the eating habits and food choices of older people and, from this data, to construct a theory of food choice specific to this age group. I recruited a self-selecting, non-random sample of 24 free-living people aged 60 years and over. With a qualitative, grounded theory approach, they were able to express their ideas with minimal influence and direction from myself. Three methods were used to collect data: semi-structured interviews, 24-hour dietary recall and seven-day food diaries. Interviews explored aspects of the food-provisioning process, such as food acquisition, as well as the wider issues surrounding food use; for example, nutritional knowledge and skill acquisition.

Data collection

Three visits were made to each person. At the first visit, I described the study and obtained informed consent to participate. Detailed demographic information and answers to some standardised questions was collected using a structured questionnaire. In addition, a 24-hour dietary recall was undertaken both as a measure of validity for the food diary, and to indicate the level of detail I was hoping for in the diary. Detailed verbal instructions were given on how to complete the diary. Further written instructions were also included in the diary.

A second shorter visit was made to collect the diary, to check on any difficulties encountered in its completion, and to make an appointment for the interview. The informal tape-recorded interview took place during the third visit.

The analysis of the transcribed interviews was assisted by NUD-IST software, with recorded incidents being identified and constantly compared. Participants were given pseudonyms (which are used below).

DIETARY MEASUREMENT: THE NUTRITIONAL SCIENCE PERSPECTIVE

The diary method of collecting data has been used in a range of academic disciplines (Scott 1990; Plummer 2001). In this paper, the nutritional science perspective is explored.

Food diaries have been used extensively by researchers interested in exploring *what* people eat. Much of this has supported a quantitative examination of the nutrients consumed by individuals, as opposed to seeking to understand the food behaviour and meanings associated with eating.

Although measurement of a person's diet appears at first to be a straightforward task, it is fraught with difficulties due to the many factors which introduce error. Measuring current diet, for example, may cause a change in behaviour but, if past diet is to be measured, then the research is dependent upon the informant's memory. Various kinds of bias may be introduced (Bingham 1991; Bingham and Nelson 1991; Bingham *et al*. 1994; Macdiarmid and Blundell 1997). For example, studies have found that obese subjects systematically under-record the amount of food they eat (Prentice *et al*. 1986). Due to the complex nature of diet, no method has been devised for collecting completely reliable and comprehensive dietary information from members of the general public (Willett 1990). Moreover, a quantitative approach requires the diets of large numbers of people to be measured; so dietary assessment methods must be relatively inexpensive.

Methods used to collect information on dietary intake include food diaries, 24-hour dietary recalls and dietary histories. Each method has advantages and disadvantages. Long-term diet, rather than intake on any specific day or small number of days, is the measurement usually required by nutritionists.

A central feature of the dietary intake of free-living individuals, is the variation from day to day, superimposed on an underlying consistent pattern (Willett 1990). A number of factors, such as day of the week or season, may systematically contribute to the daily variation in dietary intake. In practice it is often impossible to measure an individual's dietary intake for long periods of time due to the effort involved. Consequently intakes during a sample of one or more days are usually measured.

The diet record or food diary is generally designed as a special form or booklet. Subjects are taught to describe in detail the types and amounts of food or drinks they consume, to give an estimate of the quantity of food immediately before eating, and then to record any leftovers. Foods can also be weighed. Details of recipes are needed for this method if the nutrient content of the diet is to be calculated. Records are usually written, although portable tape recorders have been used. Bingham *et al.* (1995) concluded that, when validated by 24-hour urinary nitrogen, the food diary was the second best dietary assessment method, next to weighed intake. Payette and Gray-Donald (1991) found that seven-day food records were sufficiently accurate to describe the intake of a healthy older population and to demonstrate relationships of dietary intake to serum nutritional indicators.

Food diaries and their use in this study

Although nutritional analysis was not an aim of this study, food diaries were considered to be a useful tool. They enabled the participants to document their actual consumption, and to provide a record of the foods eaten. It was hoped that the diaries would show how and when food events occurred throughout the day and that they would reveal any patterns or structure.

For this study, the diaries were designed to record the types of food being eaten, the timing and spacing of meals, and relevant social information; for example, where the informant was eating and with whom. There was also space for the diarist to record other personal comments or observations. A seven day time period was selected as data could then be gathered for both week and weekend days. The diets of older people (as for other groups of the population) are influenced by day of the week (Maisey *et al.* 1995), but longer data collection periods affect data quality due to reduced compliance.

The diaries were used to provide a focus for the interview. This followed the diary-interview format described by Plummer (2001). In the interview, the diarists were asked about the information they had recorded.

The diaries were also used to validate and confirm the interview data; for example, by providing descriptive evidence of patterns of alcohol use or fruit and vegetable consumption. Comparisons could be made between the types of foods recorded (and relative financial cost) and the foods discussed in the interview. Any discrepancies could then be explored within the interview. However, if there was an under-reporting of dietary intake, as appears to be likely from previous studies (Macdiarmid and Blundell 1998), then some food items may not have been recorded.

All diaries had entries made for each day of the study. It is impossible to say whether every item of food was recorded. However, some diaries contained an incredible amount of detail and some people collected food packaging for the week, and provided supplementary information such as lists of the content of their freezer. For this study, this data was less important as it was not the intention to calculate nutrient intake or to judge the nutritional adequacy of the diets of informants.

Van Staveren *et al.* (1994) reported that food consumption studies with older people required extra equipment and time, and led to higher costs than similar studies with younger adults. None of the diarists in this study however reported any difficulty with completing the diary.

Can the use of food diaries move beyond the traditional approach of nutritionists? Can they provide information other than lists of foods that are subsequently translated into nutrients? Clues to the value of diaries lay in some of the complexities revealed which were explored in the subsequent interview. Before this I examined diaries and I used them to construct and guide my questions. For example, if it was noted that meals were always eaten at the same time, then specific questions were asked about this. Other questions prompted by the diary included: Do you always eat alone? How does this affect your diet? Why do you emphasise brand names?

I found that the data recorded in the diaries raised issues and questions which I had not anticipated. The way in which the diary and interview data were used together is explored and illustrated in the following discussion of themes emerging from the study. For a full discussion of the findings, see Dickinson (1999).

CONTENT AND CONTEXT OF MEALS

What is the social context and structure within which older people ingest nutrients? What constitutes a meal, and what is deemed to be important within this structure? We rarely choose foods for physiological reasons; rather our choices are determined by the culture in which we live (Lupton 1996). People do not eat nutrients: they eat foods.

Food ideologies describe what people think of as food. Ideologies are defined by attitudes, beliefs, customs and taboos, and thereby affect the diet of a given group (Fieldhouse 1995). Within a particular culture, not all potential foodstuffs are acceptable, some are rejected (Farb and Armelagos 1980). What is thought to be acceptable as food is an important part of the culture of a society and is passed on from generation to generation.

Social rules determine which foods constitute a particular meal, and the time of day at which it should be eaten. For example, in the UK, cereals are generally only eaten during breakfast, the first meal of the day, and three meals per day is the general pattern of food intake.

The anthropologist Mary Douglas recognised the social significance of food and eating, and attempted to decipher the codes embedded in the sequence and content of meals. She argued that eating has a social as well as a biological component, and that an analysis of food systems produces an understanding of social relations.

> Between breakfast and the last night-cap, the food of the day comes in an ordered pattern. Between Monday and Sunday, the food of the week is patterned again. Then there is the sequence of holidays and fast days throughout the year, to say nothing of life cycle feasts, birthdays and weddings. (Douglas 1997: 37)

Douglas argued that food categories encoded social events in that there is a clear idea of how they should be constituted. For example, in much of the UK, the Christmas dinner is the most elaborate meal of the year. Each week, Sunday dinner occurs as a less elaborate form of this, and other meals throughout the day and week are similarly ordered in terms of importance: 'a thick layer of meaning is accreted around every food substance' (Lupton 1996: 8).

The traditional British meal structure has been described by Nicod (1979) and Douglas and Nicod (1974). Here the 'proper' meal is based upon the three-part structure of a staple such as potato, a centrepiece of meat or fish, and one or more vegetables; these three are then covered in a 'rich brown gravy dressing'. Puddings were based on cereal, fruit and cream and are sweet. Murcott (1982) describes a similar structure for the 'cooked dinner' in South Wales and how the provision of it is an important part of women's role, and seen as vital for the health and welfare of the family.

When asked to describe what constitutes a meal, my informants provided descriptions that conformed to these rules. They made it clear that conforming to the culturally determined meal structure was very important to them. For example, they described a 'proper' meal as one that was cooked and consisted of potatoes, some kind of meat and at least one vegetable, covered with gravy, followed by a sweet course such as a pudding. This was particularly important for the Sunday meal, even for those who lived alone. The meal that conforms most closely to the structures described by Nicod is probably the Sunday dinner.

Extract 1 illustrates how the rules may be followed. At midday, Mrs Barnard had a shepherds pie with cabbage and gravy, followed by stewed apples and custard.

When other diaries were examined, however, it was apparent from the records of foods that had been eaten, that these rules are not adhered to rigidly. For example, pudding was not always eaten and, if it was, it could be a slice of cake (in which case there was no sauce). A minority did not eat a roast dinner on Sunday, and women who lived alone were less likely to conform to these mealtime structures. Mrs Crabtree, for example, who now lives alone after being widowed, described what was important about a meal for her and went on to explain how this was different on a Sunday.

Extract 1: Monday in Mrs Barnard's diary.

Time	Food and drink consumed	Where and with whom
5.45am	2 cups of tea, 1 Marie biscuit	In kitchen with radio on
8am	Cooked 2 tablespoons of Quaker oats. Had them with milk and brown sugar, 1 slice of toast and marmalade.	In kitchen; radio still on
9am to 12pm		Made orange cake, also Yorkshire Parkin for granddaughter and family, also lemon cake for self
12pm	Frozen shepherds pie from freezer with 2 tablespoons of cabbage and gravy Pudding: stewed apples and custard	
2pm		Not much on TV Read magazines
5.30pm	Piece of toast with cheese put on melted under grill 1 cup of tea	
10.45pm	Coffee made with milk and water	
11.15pm		Went to bed

How would you describe a typical meal at lunchtime?

Well just meat and vegetables, gravy, potatoes, a couple or three veg. I do like veg and I have two or three veg every day and whatever, either pie, sausages or a chop or something like that, you know. Sundays I bother a bit more ... Well I'd roast the potatoes, and do perhaps an extra veg and might have a pudding or something on a Sunday. Then I don't eat very much after Sunday at all then because I've had a bit more at dinnertime. I might just have a cup of tea and a piece of cake or something at teatime then. ... We've always had a bigger meal on a Sunday lunch time, I suppose, always had a roast on a Sunday sort of thing and, a habit really. ... I'd have a lamb chop or pork chop or piece of chicken or something like that ... I don't bother with roast during the week. [004: 634-667]

This excerpt reveals the extra effort she puts into preparing her Sunday lunch when compared with weekday meals. Other lunches that she recorded during the diary week included:

Monday: 2 sausages, portion mashed potato, cabbage. No pudding.

Thursday: Small tin of soup (vegetable). Apple.

Friday: Fish and potato cake (frozen), peas. Half a grapefruit.

Extract 2 shows that her Sunday lunch included roast meat, extra vegetables and a pudding.

According to their diaries, the majority of the interviewees had a more elaborate meal on the Sunday. This entailed 'more bother' and took more time to prepare. It usually included roast elements such as roast meat, even if this was a chop and not a joint of meat. Other studies have found a similar variation in the nutrient intake of older people associated with the day of the week and, in particular, Sundays. This can be explained by the importance placed upon the Sunday dinner by members of this older generation (Maisey *et al*. 1995; Finch *et al*. 1998).

The 'proper' cooked meal can be contrasted with the lighter meal that is often described as 'a snack'. Mrs Barnard, having described what constitutes a proper cooked meal for her, commented that a snack does not fill her up in the same way as a proper meal. The role of the proper meal extends beyond the material and nutritional: it can be seen to fill

Extract 2: Sunday in Mrs Crabtree's diary

Time	Food and drink consumed	Where and with whom
8am	2 mugs of tea, 2 biscuits 1 orange	At home alone
11am	Mug of coffee	
12.30pm	Lamb chop, small potato 4 Brussels Small carrot and parsnip Small portion of Xmas Pudding	
5pm	2 slices of bread and butter. Cake	
9pm	Small Sherry	
10.30pm	Mug of milk	

her up metaphorically as well as physically. In this way, a 'proper meal' has significant cultural meaning:

> If I don't have a cooked meal, I don't feel the same. I feel there's something missing. I don't know why. You know, I feel as if, well say at lunchtime, and I just have say something, spaghetti on toast, or baked beans on toast. Say if I'm in a hurry, I'm going somewhere, and I haven't had a proper meal, I don't feel the same. I feel so hungry when I come home at teatime. And then I feel I've got to have a fry-up, egg, bacon and chips, and things like that. Because I've really missed my meal at lunchtime then.

> So you mentioned, you called it a proper meal, what do you mean by a proper meal? What would be included in that?

> Meat and two veg, and gravy, you know, like that. Potatoes, yes, always potatoes, yes. And nearly always a pudding. [006: 1210-1224]

This structure of the 'proper' meal reflects those described by Murcott (1982) and by Charles and Kerr (1988) in their studies of food and women with young children. This is not surprising as women in these studies will have inherited cultural knowledge from the women of the generations represented in my study.

Meals are often eaten at regular times of day, consisting of breakfast and, generally, one 'proper' meal and a 'snack' or lighter meal. Here is Mrs Owen's description:

> Well, we get mostly, I get breakfast any time from half past eight to nine. And then lunch any time after half past twelve. And if we're in, we get a cup of tea at fourish. And then supper at sixish, or after .... We usually get one substantial meal and one more snacky meal. But it doesn't matter which if we get a substantial lunch, we get a snacky supper, the other way round ... I don't call a meal a real meal unless it's got potato in it. [019: 660-666]

For Mrs Owen, a 'snacky' meal tends to be based on bread rather than potatoes:

> Well, say cuppa soup, with bread and cheese. Or just bread and cheese, perhaps with tomato. Or maybe a tuna sandwich or a boiled egg ... It's some kind of protein with bread. [019: 712-716]

Extract 3 illustrates the three meals in Mrs Owen's day. Note the lighter meal at midday and the 'proper meal' in the early evening.

Significant variations with age have been found in other studies of older people: younger people having a less 'traditional' diet than those who were older (Finch *et al.* 1998). Similarly I found that the rules which govern what is an acceptable component of a meal incorporate some less traditionally British foods such as pasta and rice among some of the younger informants, replacing the staple of potato. The Sunday dinner however continues to be based on a traditional roast.

The description outlined above is included in part to set the context of the eating habits of older people. In addition it indicates that the cultural importance of the structure and content of meals should be considered when any dietary 'improvement' is planned through health education or promotion for *any* group of the population. As Nicod concludes:

The local food system needs to be understood and appreciated in the context of its interlinkage with the family and other social institutions within the community if any efforts to improve dietary intake are not to meet resistance from the people themselves. (1979: 64)

Extract 3: Monday in Mrs Owen's diary.

Time	Food and drink consumed	Where and with whom
8.45am	2 slices wholemeal bread, butter and marmalade 2 inches of banana 1 mug tea	Living room with radio
12.30pm	Chicken mayonnaise sandwich 2 shortbread fingers 2oz jelly babies 2 mugs of tea	In Centre (voluntary work)
4.00pm	2 mugs tea	Living room with husband
6.30pm	2 oz steak, small portion oven chips, mixed veg 1 Lion bar 1 mug of tea	Ditto
11.00pm	2 cups of tea	Ditto

THREE MEALS A DAY? THE SOCIAL SIGNIFICANCE OF MEALTIMES

For these women, meals tend to be eaten at regular intervals, with patterns of mealtimes changing very little from day to day. Often these times were set earlier in their lives to suit their lifestyles. For example, they may have prepared the midday meal for the time when their husband came home from work and their children arrived home from school. Many continued with this routine even though the reason for the timing no longer existed. In maintaining these set patterns of eating, meaningful structure is added to the day when paid employment no longer provides routine to the day and the week.

Not eating at the usual time can be problematic. Mrs Morris for example explained how she avoids eating meals at the home of her daughter, as they eat later than she prefers and is used to. Many years ago she timed the preparation of the main meal for the arrival home of her husband and daughter, and she continues to eat her main meal at the same time. It is important for her to maintain a routine:

> But I do make sure I have a main meal at lunchtime. I could go up to [my daughter's] but you see they don't have their Sunday lunch till three o'clock. If I left it till three o'clock I just wouldn't be hungry, because I've always had lunch at lunchtime. Because both her and her dad, even when he was at work and she was at school, they always came home for lunch you see ... About twelve, half past twelve, one. [001: 116-123]

Mrs Thomas also eats at regular times and explains how she feels faint if she does not eat regularly:

> I mean even if I'm out, I goes out the other week, where was I, oh I was out with my son, and I said to him, I said I've gotta get home my duck, my legs are trembling, I haven't eaten and I've gotta get home and eat.... Mostly I suppose my weeks are doing, my days are more or less much the same going through, but even if I'm out for the day, anywhere, always stop and eat, have something at that time. [021: 899-912]

Others describe regular eating as important to their health. For example, two of the people interviewed described how they had to eat regularly as they had hiatus hernias. They had been advised by their doctor to eat small meals at regular intervals.

Mrs Eaden, in contrast, has failed to establish a mealtime routine since she was widowed a year ago. Her diary indicates that her diet could be suffering as a result of this, she often misses meals and tends to rely frequently on snacks of cakes and bars of chocolate (Extract 4).

Extract 4: Friday in Mrs Eaden's diary

Time	Food and drink consumed	Where and with whom
8am	2 cups of tea, milk and 2 sugars per cup. 2 slices of brown bread sandwich, cold turkey filling	In kitchen, doing jobs
12 mid-day	1 packet of salt & vinegar crisps	In friend's kitchen
4pm	1 rocky chocolate sandwich biscuits 1 cup of tea, with milk and 2 sugars	At daughter's home
5.30pm	1 fruit scone with spread	At home, in kitchen alone
8pm	Jacket potato, with spread and spaghetti (tinned) Fruit cocktail with custard (tinned)	In sitting room, alone watching TV
Midnight	Drinking chocolate (fat reduced) mug with 2 sugars, milk, water Mini chocolate Easter Egg	Getting ready for bed

Since I'm on my own, no plans, you know. I, er, do my own thing, so basically no plans, you know. The rare day I probably do plan, but not very often.

Did you before your husband died?

Yes, yes. I mean sometimes I'm eating here at eight o'clock at night whereas when, well up until the time he retired, we got a bit sort of flexible then, but before that, I mean we were eating about five o'clock your meal about five, five half past, six o'clock and that was it, but I mean when he retired, as I say, he was 67 when he retired, and he was 85 when he died, so we had nearly 20 years of it, but I mean we still kept, I kept to as near time as possible for the evening meal, but as I say now, no, sometimes I'm sitting here and [my friend] rings and she says 'Are you eating?', you know. She says 'I never know when to ring you whether you're gonna sort of, your meal's nearly ready or something', so basically no plans, no plans at all, being on your own. [017: 594-611]

EATING ALONE

Commensality is defined as the social significance of eating together (Morrison 1996). Highlighting the cultural norm of commensality, the Health and Lifestyle Survey (Health Education Authority 1998) found that 95 per cent of respondents were eating with others.

What is striking about the food diaries of those who live alone is that they eat the majority, if not all, of their food alone. The companionship of others is replaced by the radio or television set. The stark social context of their mealtimes contrasts with the importance placed by others on eating together as couples or families. It is perhaps unsurprising then that for some older people who live alone, the meal becomes unimportant and eating becomes a purely functional act divorced from its sociability.

The meal as an event can be diminished when it no longer contains a social component. There is a disintegration of the accepted social behaviour attached to the settings of meals, such as eating at the table, a part of the meal occasion that is given much importance by couples and families (Charles and Kerr 1988). Ultimately this disintegration may extend to the structure and content of the meal itself. A lack of routine with regard to meals and eating could be used as an indicator of nutritional risk.

CONCLUSION

This analysis has adopted a functional structural approach in the style of Douglas (1997) and Murcott (1982), but this approach is not without its critics (e.g. Mennell et al. 1992). What it has revealed is how the structure of meals is important to older people, and how the rules governing these structures are not as rigid as previously thought, particularly among the younger cohort of older people. Gradual historical changes in the diets of older people are occurring, highlighting further the heterogeneity that exists among older people and the constantly changing cultural context of meals. Also it has shown how rules are broken when people no longer perceive them to be important and, in particular, when they live alone.

The analysis has shown how food diaries provide us with more than lists of foods to be translated into nutrients. Rather they provide clues to the symbolic aspects of food and eating, and how the very individual experiences of older people are influenced by their biographies. As such, diaries are a useful tool with which to investigate daily activities such as eating. The data they produce is enhanced further when the documented activities are explored using the interview method. Although this study is based on a small sample, there appears to be a strong correlation between what actually happens (as recorded within a short time of the event) and what older people describe in interviews as happening.

REFERENCES

Bingham, S. (1991) Limitations of the various methods for collecting dietary intake data, *Annals of Nutrition and Metabolism* 35: 117–127.

Bingham, S.A. and Nelson, M. (1991) Assessment of food consumption and nutrient intake, in Margetts, B.M. and Nelson, M. (eds) *Design Concepts in Nutritional Epidemiology*, Oxford University Press, New York, pp. 153–191.

Bingham, S.A., Gill, C., Welch, A., Day, K., Cassidy, A., Khaw, K.T., Sneyd, M.J., Key, T.J.A., Roe, L. and Day, N.E. (1994) Comparison of dietary assessment methods in nutritional epidemiology: weighed records v 24 hour recalls, food-frequency questionnaires and estimated-diet records, *British Journal of Nutrition* 72: 619–643.

Bingham, S.A., Cassidy, A., Cole, T.J., Welch, A., Runswick, S.A., Black, A.E., Thurnham, D., Bates, C., Khaw, K.T., Key, T.J.A. and Day, N.E. (1995) Validation of weighed records and other methods of dietary assessment using the 24 hour urine nitrogen technique and other biological markers, *British Journal of Nutrition*, 73: 531–550.

Charles, N. and Kerr, M. (1988) *Women, Food and Families*, Manchester University Press, Manchester.

Dickinson, A. (1999) *Food Choice and Eating Habits of Older People: A Grounded Theory*, unpublished PhD Thesis, Buckinghamshire Chilterns University College, Brunel University.

Douglas, M. (1997) Deciphering a meal, in Counihan, C. and Van Esterik, P. (eds) *Food and Culture – a Reader*, Routledge, New York, pp. 36–54.

Douglas, M. and Nicod, N. (1974) Taking the biscuit; the structure of British meals, *New Society* 30 (637): 744–747.

Farb, P. and Armelagos, G. (1980) *Consuming Passions – The Anthropology of Eating*, Houghton Mifflin, Boston.

Fieldhouse, P. (1995) *Food and Nutrition – Customs and Culture*, 2nd edition, Chapman & Hall, London.

Finch, S., Doyle, W., Lowe, C., Bates, C.J., Prentice, A., Smithers, G. and Clarke, P.C. (1998) *National Diet and Nutrition Survey: People Aged 65 Years and Over*, The Stationery Office, London.

Germov, J. and Williams, L. (1996) The epidemic of dieting women: the need for a sociological approach to food and nutrition, *Appetite* 27: 97–108.

Health Education Authority (1998) *The HEA Health and Lifestyle Survey. A report on the secondary analysis of a national dataset of health-related knowledge, attitudes and behaviour*, HEA, London.

Lupton, D. (1996) *Food, the Body and the Self*, Sage, London.

Macdiarmid, J.I. and Blundell, J.E. (1997) Dietary under-reporting: what people say about recording their food intake, *European Journal of Clinical Nutrition* 51(3): 199–200.

Macdiarmid, J.I. and Blundell, J.E. (1998) Assessing dietary intake: who, what and why of under-reporting, *Nutrition Research Reviews* 11(2): 231–253.

Maisey, S., Loughridge, J., Southon, S. and Fulcher, R. (1995) Variation in food group and nutrient intake with day of the week in an elderly population, *British Journal of Nutrition* 73: 359–373.

Mennell, S., Murcott, A. and van Otterloo, A.H. (1992) *The Sociology of Food, Eating, Diet and Culture*, Sage, London.

Morrison, M. (1996) Sharing food at home and at school: perspectives on commensality, *The Sociological Review* 44: 648–674.

Murcott, A. (1982) On the social significance of the cooked dinner in South Wales, *Social Science Information* 21(4/5): 677–696.

Nicod, M. (1979) Gastronomically speaking: food studied as a medium of communication, in Turner, M. (ed.) *Nutrition and Lifestyles*, Applied Science Publishers, Barking, Essex, pp. 53–65.

Payette, H. and Gray-Donald, K. (1991) Dietary intake and biochemical indices of nutritional status in an elderly population, with estimates of the precision of the 7-d food record, *American Journal of Clinical Nutrition* 54: 478–488.

Plummer, K. (2001) *Documents of Life 2: An Invitation to Critical Humanism,* Sage, London.

Prentice, A.M., Black, A.E., Coward, W.A., Davies, H.L., Goldberg, G.R., Murgatroyd, P.R., Ashford, J., Sawyer, M. and Whitehead, R.G. (1986) High levels of energy expenditure in obese women, *British Medical Journal* 292: 983–987.

Scott, J. (1990) *A Matter of Record: Documentary Sources in Social Research,* Polity Press, Cambridge.

van Staveren, W.A., de Groot, L.C.P.G.M., Blauw, Y.H. and van der Wielden, R.P.J. (1994) Assessing diets of elderly people: problems and approaches, *American Journal of Clinical Nutrition* 59 (Suppl): 221S–223S.

Willett, W. (1990) *Nutritional Epidemiology,* Oxford University Press, Oxford.